BROWN-OUT & SLOW-DOWN

BROWN-
OUT
&

RICHARD SALTONSTALL JR.
AND JAMES K. PAGE JR.

SLOW-
DOWN

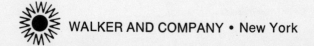

WALKER AND COMPANY • New York

First published in the United States of America in 1972 by the Walker Publishing Company, Inc.

Published simultaneously in Canada by Fitzhenry & Whiteside, Limited, Toronto.

ISBN: 0-8027-0365-8

Library of Congress Catalog Card Number: 71-179613

Printed in the United States of America.

CONTENTS

Letter to the Honorable John V. Lindsay
from Charles F. Luce July 22, 1969. En-
vironmental Protection Checklist and
Guidelines for Site Selection (from
ELECTRIC POWER AND THE ENVIRONMENT,
U.S. Office of Technology).

BIBLIOGRAPHY

To whomever it was who made the first windmill, and to BARON KARL VON DRAIS, *inventor in 1816 of the bicycle.*

PART I

ENERGY

CHAPTER 1

WHO NEEDS
ENERGY?

Energy is the capacity for performing work—any kind of work such as the growth of a plant, the plowing of a field, or the turning of a wheel. Throughout most of human history and even throughout much of the world today, the energy needed to do man's work has been provided by the exertion of his own muscles and the muscles of the animals he has domesticated. This fact is evident in the use of such words as *manpower* and *horsepower*. To be sure, ancient men used the tides and winds to drive their fragile boats; they harnessed free-falling water to turn crude wheels. But the creation of Western industrial civilization can be attributed, in great part, to the rise of new and more powerful forms of energy to do man's work.

The steam engine of the 17th Century was surely a monumental breakthrough. However, the real watershed to the present may have occurred just before the turn of the 20th Century when a prescient American historian named Henry Adams stood before one of the first large dynamos and forecast that this would be the object and the symbol around which the 20th Century would organize itself. Adams was right. Electric power, and the uses we have put it to, are at the center of our civilization and, also, at the center of one of our civilization's most severe dilemmas—the crisis in energy resources.

The use of electrical power in the United States has doubled during *each* of the past three decades. This is an average increase of seven percent each year for thirty years. And in recent years, the rate of electrical consumption rose slightly *over* seven percent a year. The increasing demand is not primarily a function of population growth, though the addition of more and more people aggravates the situation. The key to the increased demand lies in the fact that the per capita consumption of electricity in the U.S. has increased five times as much as our population. If everyone in the world used as much power as we do, the presently known reserves of fuel to produce the power would be exhausted within eighteen months.

The combustion of fuels is needed not only to produce electricity, but also for transportation, industrial processes and heating buildings. At present, the fuels used to produce all this energy consist almost entirely of coal, oil, various forms of gas, and uranium. It took millions of years for the organic material buried under the ground to evolve into fossil fuels—coal, oil, and natural gas. These resources, and uranium as well, are finite: they will run out. The question is when, and the answer, while never precise, is always discomforting.

In a a recent paper in a National Academy of Sciences report called *Resources and Man,* M. King Hubbert of the United States Geological Survey predicted that the earth's coal supply might be made to last as long as three or four centuries, but that it would last only half that period if man continues to use coal as a major source of energy production. The use of petroleum, Hubbert forecasts, will peak in the early decades of the next century and world oil deposits will be depleted within eighty years from now. Natural gas production will peak within two decades, according to available evidence, and in the same period we will begin to suffer from a shortage of Uranium-235, the present source of nuclear power.

These estimates strike a balance between the most optimistic and the most pessimistic of many such forecasts. Yet public officials, resource-using industries and, not least, the public have all looked with blithe faith into the future. We seem to have been lulled by the extraordinary technological changes of our time into assuming that around every corner there is another technological breakthrough. But before previous breakthroughs, scientists have usually been able to predict with some certainty the range of options and future possibilities. This is not the case in the energy crisis.

The methods presently being counted on to meet our future electrical needs are either not yet very promising or they are largely untested. The gasification of coal, new nuclear reactors, fusion power, solar energy, the harnessing of the winds and the tides, and the release of energy from beneath the earth's crust through continental drift all provide interesting speculation— but, for now at least, not a great deal more.

These future hopes will be explored later in this book; meanwhile, the energy crisis is with us now. This is evident to anyone whose air conditioning has been shut off when a utility announces that reduction in energy consumption is mandatory. And the production of energy, as more and more people are beginning to understand, is leading to a host of environmental problems (see Chapter II). First, however, let us examine some statistics on who is using all the electricity and how much is being used.

Who Uses Power—and How Much?

In the U.S., industry consumes less than one-third of the fuel that is required for energy; electric utilities use less than one-fourth; transportation just over one-fourth, and households and other consumers about one-fourth. So industry is the 'hog.' In a recent report (see Bibliography), three distinguished scientists, Barry Commoner, Michael Corr and Paul J. Stamler, held that *modern industrial processes* are mostly to blame for environmental pollution and sheer wastefulness in the use of energy. These authors pointed out that, in the U.S., the population has grown forty-eight percent since 1946 while the Gross National Product has grown fifty-nine percent. In the same years, the level of pollution has increased many times over. This led them to conclude that environmental excesses are caused mainly by new methods of production, notably the use of new chemicals and synthetics, and by a tremendous rise in the use of energy to convert resources into new products. For example, cotton at one time was widely used in fabrics. The energy expended in arriving at this product came naturally through photosynthesis. New synthetic fabrics require a much higher expenditure of energy since they are chemically extracted or combined from natural resources. Plastic used to be made from cellulose. Now it comes from a variety of synthetics. An aluminum can requires the use of many times more energy than a can made from steel.

Industries' demand for their own manufacturing energy grows and will continue to grow until such excesses are penalized by new laws. But the crisis that has most completely galvanized public concern has been the growing shortage of electricity produced by the nation's utilities. As we have noted, the true gravity of the shortage—limitations on resources and the lack of alternatives—does not yet seem to be appreciated. But the public is well aware that the utilities want more power to keep up with demand. Most large cities have experienced, during hot summer months, those severe voltage shortages called brownouts and who can forget the great blackout in the Northeast in 1965? Everyday, somewhere, there is a battle in progress over the siting of a power plant.

The source of the problem is simple to pinpoint: the extravagant living habits of Americans who keep right on using more and more electricity. In addition, new sewage plants, waste recycling systems and other environmental controls, as well as cleaner transportation—notably rapid transit—will certainly require more electricity. Thus, the focus of the discussion in Part I of this book is on energy for electricity. It is an area in which citizen concern and citizen action can have great effects.

A report by the Energy Policy Staff of the Office of Science and Technology in December, 1968, (see Bibliography) noted that U.S. electrical generating capacity totalled just under 300,000 megawatts or 300,000,000 kilowatts. It was then estimated that nearly 500 new power plants of varying size and type would have to be built by 1990 in order to meet the country's projected need for just over one million megawatts of generating capacity.

Expressed differently, the present gross annual use of 1.52 trillion kilowatt-hours of electricity is expected to increase 284 percent to 5.83 trillion kilowatt-hours in 1990.

TABLE 1: U.S. ELECTRIC UTILITY REQUIREMENTS
AND SUPPLY[1], 1965-90

	1965	1970	1980	1990
Energy requirement (trillion kilowatt-hours)	1.06	1.52	3.07	5.83
Peak demand (million kilowatt-hours)....	188.0	277.0	554.0	1,051.0
Total installed capacity (million kilowatt-hours)......................	236.1	344.0	668.0	1,261.0
Hydroelectric capacity (million kilowatt-hours)	41.7	51.4	68.0	83.0
Pumped storage capacity (million kilowatt-hours)	1.3	3.6	24.0	65.1
Internal combustion and gas turbine capacity (million kilowatt-hours)	4.9	16.2	27.0	42.0
Fossil steam capacity (million kilowatt-hours)	187.5	261.2	399.0	562.0
Nuclear capacity (million kilowatt-hours) .	.7	11.6	150.0	509.0
Capacity dependent on cooling water (in million kilowatt-hours)..............	188.2	272.8	549.0	1,071.0

SOURCE: Federal Power Commission
[1]Excludes Alaska and Hawaii

Per capita consumption of electricity in the U.S. has reached 10,000 watts per day and is growing 2.5 percent annually. The annual kilowatt-hour per capita use of electricity has risen from 540 in 1920 to 7,950 in 1970. It is projected to rise to 22,200 by 1990.

How Electricity Is Made

How is all this electricity produced? As the 1970s began, the greatest amount was generated in steam turbines. The steam comes from boilers that were heated by coal, oil or uranium.

At the electric plant, steam is produced by boiling water. The steam is then forced into turbines at extremely high pressures. The turbines drive generators that produce electricity. The problem that all steam plants have in common is how to dispose of waste heat that develops *before* and *during* the steam cycle. A conventional steam plant (i.e. one that uses fossil fuel) can produce about two units of heat for every three that are wasted. This means it has an efficiency of forty percent. A nuclear plant operates at only thirty percent efficiency, delivering about one unit of heat for electricity while wasting two units. Moreover, the closed system of the nuclear plant (see p. 34-41) requires up to fifty percent more cooling water to recondense steam. The conventional plants get rid of about a fifth of their waste heat by sending it up the combustion stack in various forms, contributing greatly to air pollution as will be explained in Chapter 2. Nuclear plants dispose of all their waste heat into the lake, river or estuary from which they draw cooling water for their condensing stage.

All electric plants are voracious users of water. A one-million kilowatt nuclear plant, typical of those now being built or planned, will use 850,000 gallons a minute, over one billion gallons a day. The 1968 Energy Policy Staff report noted that "By 1980 the electricity power industry will require about one-sixth of the total available fresh water runoff in the entire nation for cooling purposes." By 2000, that percentage is supposed to double. It would be ideal if towns and cities were run as efficiently as naval ships, which make use of almost all the waste heat from their steam boilers by using it to run auxiliary systems, to produce fresh water and to heat the living and working spaces. But, unfortunately, our communities are not as simple as ships.

Hydroelectric power. The first electrical power produced in this nation, and from an environmental standpoint the cleanest, came from hydroelectric projects, the best known of which are the Hoover and Grand Coulee Dams. For centuries, water had been used in mills to drive saws and looms and to grind food. It was only logical that falling water be used to push the turbines of an electric plant. Hydroelectric plants produce no air or water pollution, no radioactive contamination and no noise, the last being an objection to gas turbines. At present, they generate nearly fifteen percent of the nation's electricity or 51,400 megawatts of the 344,000 megawatts available in 1970. However, there are very real limitations on hydroelectric power. For one thing, with an exception like Niagara Falls, there are few natural river sites in the U.S. where large amounts of power can be produced. Most large hydroelectric projects have been created by building dams behind which great volumes of water are stored. Thus, hydroelectric projects disrupt the free-flowing characteristics of rivers, destroy scenic values and often produce a variety of adverse ecological side effects more fully discussed in Chapter 2. It suffices to say now that plans for the nation's future power needs do not include significant increases in the hydroelectric output. Far greater use is expected to be made of falling water in what are known as pumped storage hydroelectric projects. In these plants, fuel-powered generators are used in off-hours to pump water from a lake or river into an elevated basin. Then, during peak hours, the water is released through turbines. However, as we will later point out, this concept is also not free from ecological consequences.

TABLE 2: PROJECTION OF GENERATING CAPACITY

On the basis of the 1970 National Power Survey peak demand projection, a tentative estimate of the mix of generating facilities by types for 1980 and 1990 is as follows:

	1970		1980		1990	
	Megawatts	Percent	Megawatts	Percent	Megawatts	Percent
Conventional hydro	51,400	14.9	68,000	10.2	81,945	6.5
Pumped storage hydro	3,600	1.1	27,000	4.0	70,000	5.5
Fossil steam	261,200	75.9	396,000	59.3	559,000	43.3
Internal combustion and gas turbine	16,200	4.7	30,000	4.5	50,000	4.0
Nuclear	11,600	3.4	147,000	22.0	500.000	39.7
TOTAL	344,000	100.0	668,000	100.0	1,260,945	100.0

SOURCE: Federal Power Commission

Coal.   Coal, which accounts for slightly less than sixty percent of present U.S. power production, cannot be mined fast enough to meet projected energy requirements unless great changes occur in both the market and the methods of extraction. At present 297,000,000 tons of coal are used annually in the U.S. to generate electricity. If, by the year 2000, the use of coal as a source of electric energy were to account for only thirty percent of U.S. electricity generation, over one billion tons will have to be mined each year. But if coal were to continue its present role in energy production, some six million tons of coal would be consumed *daily*. This would involve, among other things, the daily movement of 60,000 railroad cars, a logistical absurdity. In the past several years, coal-burning utilities have been hard pressed to keep a month's supply of coal in their yards.

In addition, the costs of labor, long overdue health and safety laws affecting mining, air and water pollution codes and regulations in strip mining have combined to make coal expensive. It is clear that if coal reserves are to be tapped in the future to produce electricity, the resource will undoubtedly have to be used to a large extent in liquid or gas form, about which more will be said in Chapter 4.

Oil.   The fuel oil picture is no brighter. For one thing, since it is not economical to move oil long distances over land (e.g. by pipeline), the use of oil by utilities is limited largely to coastal regions near refineries and deep water ports. New techniques have become available to lower the sulfur content in oil, thus making it environmentally more acceptable. But the supply, as indicated earlier, is limited over the long term and other environmental considerations, such as the risk of oil spills from ships and offshore drilling operations, make residual fuel oil less and less attractive as a fuel for electricity.

TABLE 3: PROJECTION OF FUEL USE FOR STEAM-ELECTRIC
POWER GENERATION

On the basis of the anticipated competitive position of the various electric utility fuels during the next two decades, the 1970 National Power Survey projects the use of the various fuels expressed in equivalent tons of coal having a heat equivalent of 25 million Btu as follows:

	1970		1980		1990	
	Tons (Millions)	Percent	Tons	Percent	Tons	Percent
Coal	304.6	56.7	472.0	42.5	613.6	28.8
Gas	145.9	27.2	195.9	17.2	245.9	11.6
Oil	59.5	11.1	86.8	7.8	91.8	4.3
Nuclear	27.2	5.0	356.5	32.1	1,176.1	55.3
TOTAL	537.2	100.0	1,111.2	100.0	2,127.4	100.0

The most important change anticipated in thermal generation of electric power indicated by the 1970 National Power Survey is the extraordinary growth expected in nuclear generation during the next two decades. In 1990, nuclear generation is expected to account for 55 percent of the electric energy requirements of that year, an increase of more than 40 times the nuclear generation expected in 1970.

SOURCE: Federal Power Commission

Natural gas. In recent years, particularly to meet peak load demands, utilities have resorted to gas turbines fueled by natural gas or light oil. Gas turbines are like jet aircraft engines. The turbine blades are driven by the expansion of high-pressure gases resulting from fuel combustion. Typically, they are small units, no larger than fifty megawatts (one-twentieth the size of a typical nuclear plant), and their efficiency is seldom greater than twenty-five percent. All their waste heat goes into the atmosphere.

In the short term, particularly because of its desirability as a clean fuel, utilities are counting heavily on natural gas to help meet peak load demands for power. In 1968, more than 3.1 trillion cubic feet of natural gas provided twenty-three percent of the nation's power or twenty-seven percent of U.S. thermal power, excluding hydroelectricity. Nearly half this gas was consumed in Texas and California. And yet, while growth of natural gas is expected to increase to 33.5 percent during this decade, it will drop sharply thereafter, to 4.8 percent of thermal power by 2000.

As this book was written, a controversy raged over the pricing of natural gas and the question of whether there were sufficient incentives to spur the discovery of gas reserves. The FPC allowed gas suppliers to raise their prices. This resulted in an outcry that the agency had either been misled concerning the long-term gas shortage or was being cozy with the gas producers. In any event, it is clear that consumption of natural gas cannot long climb at its present rate of seven percent a year. According to a *Wall Street Journal* report, at present rate of use, natural gas reserves will not last longer than sixty-eight years.

The virtual exhaustion of the earth's fuel resources is an awesome matter to contemplate: it is the worst of many problems in the dilemma of power, but there are others that are with us even now.

CHAPTER 2

ENVIRONMENTAL
LIABILITIES

Until we learn to harness the energy of the sun on a mass scale—and perhaps not even then—there will be no such thing as *clean* power. Even worse, no present single method of generating electricity has clear-cut advantages over the others. A complex variety of conditions dictates which method of generating power is cleaner in a given place at a given time. "The environmental and health and safety problems seem to play no favorites in the energy field," S. David Freeman, former director of the Energy Policy Staff of the Office of Science and Technology, said in a speech in 1969. He added that "Environmental concerns pose a new and overriding challenge to which all energy systems must address themselves."

So far, the nation's utilities have faltered badly, playing a very weak game of catch-up ball. Most of them still advertise the benefits of using more electricity while at the same time they anguish before public service commissions and the increasingly conservation-conscious citizenry, claiming that they need more and bigger power plants to keep up with the demand for electricity. Of course, it doesn't make sense.

What are the environmental liabilities of generating power?

Effects on Water

It is worth repeating that at the present rate of growth, U.S. utilities will use one-sixth of the nation's fresh water flow by 1980 and one-third by the turn of the century to cool their steam plant condensers. Most U.S. power plants employ "once-through" cooling techniques whereby water is taken from the sea or a body of fresh water. This water, called thermal discharge or thermal addition is, on the average, fifteen degrees hotter than the water from which it came and to which it returns.

The hot water significantly affects the breeding, feeding and maturation cycles of fish and smaller aquatic organisms. Warmer water contains less oxygen, but fish in warmer water demand more oxygen. Meanwhile, the warmer water encourages the growth of algae that also use oxygen, thus reducing a waterway's capacity to assimilate oxygen-demanding wastes. Dr. Donald Mount, director of the Federal Water Quality Laboratory in Duluth, Minnesota, has shown that slight temperature changes usually have an adverse affect on fish. For example, minnows, the main food of sport and commercial fish, suffer a twenty-five percent loss in reproductive capacity with a temperature rise from seventy-two to seventy-nine degrees Fahrenheit. In the range of eighty-six to ninety-five degrees, green algae thrive. Above ninety-five degrees, blue-green algae take over and cause a bad odor and taste in the water. In recent years, government biologists have blamed thermal pollution from electric plants for massive fish kills in rivers and estuaries throughout the country, from the Columbia to the Hudson, in Puget Sound and Biscayne Bay.

TABLE 4: MINIMUM AND MAXIMUM TEMPERATURES FOR CERTAIN FRESHWATER FISHES

Fish	Acclimated To °C	Acclimated To °F	Minimum Temperature[1] °C	Minimum Temperature[1] °F	Minimum Temperature[1] Time, Hr.	Maximum Temperature °C	Maximum Temperature °F	Maximum Temperature Time, Hr.
Bass, largemouth	20.0	68.0	5.0	41.0	24	32.0	89.6	72
	30.0	86.0	11.0	51.8	24	34.0	93.2	72
Bluegill (*Lepomis*	15.0	59.0	3.0	37.4	24	31.0	87.8	60
macrochirus purpurescens)	30.0	86.0	11.0	51.8	24	34.0	93.2	60

Fish	Acclimated To °C	°F	Minimum Temperature[1] °C	°F	Time, Hr.	Maximum Temperature °C	°F	Time, Hr.
Catfish, channel	15.0	59.0	0.0	32.0	24	30.0	86.0	24
	25.0	77.0	6.0	42.8	24	34.0	93.2	24
Perch, yellow	5.0	41.0	----	----	--	21.0	69.8	96
(Winter)	25.0	77.0	4.0	39.2	24	30.0	86.0	96
(Summer)	25.0	77.0	9.0	48.2	24	32.0	89.6	96
Shad, gizzard	25.0	77.0	11.0	51.8	24	34.0	93.2	48
	35.0	95.0	20.0	68.0	24	37.0	98.6	48
Shiner, common	5.0	41.0	----	----	--	27.0	80.6	133
(Notropis cornutus	25.0	77.0	4.0	39.2	24	31.0	87.8	133
frontalis)	30.0	86.0	8.0	46.4	24	31.0	87.8	133
Trout, brook	3.0	37.4	----	----	--	23.0	73.4	133
	20.0	68.0	----	----	--	25.0	77.0	133

SOURCE: Industrial Waste Guide on Thermal Pollution

[1]Values are LD$_{50}$ temperature tolerance limits, i.e., water temperatures survived by 50 percent of the test fish.

Recent studies by government and university scientists are beginning to show that fish can suffer a variety of ill effects at temperatures below those that are immediately lethal to them but above their normal temperature range. In water at sublethal temperatures, fish have a reduced resistance to various diseases. Nonetheless, a waterway might adjust to thermal changes, or a tolerant fish population might evolve under the warmer conditions, if the thermal addition was stable. But this is not the case. A steam plant's influence on a waterway varies according to the electric load. There are peaks and there are slack periods.

So far there has been little effort in either the private or public sectors to explore beneficial uses of thermal addition, for example, the possibilities of cycling warm water through irrigation systems and desalinization units. In addition, there has been no progress in making the steam cycle more efficient so that generator turbines can use steam at varying lower temperatures.

Cooling ponds and towers. For the present, cooling ponds and cooling towers are the only technically and economically feasible remedies for thermal pollution. Ponds are the preferred solution where the land is available at low cost. They are cheaper to operate and there is less evaporative loss of water. However, there are very few areas where the land is cheap enough to build a pond that takes up to one thousand acres or more.

There are in general three kinds of cooling towers: mechanical forced draft, hyperbolic natural draft and dry. The mechanical towers (see p. 17-19) incorporate fans which blow air through a heat transfer system into which hot water is drawn by pipes or is sprayed. The hyperbolic towers, so-called because of their profile, feature natural cooling and high evaporation as cool air is blown under the hot water, resulting in water vapor that rises out of the tower. Dry towers have been used successfully in England but so far none have yet been built in the U.S.

The following table was presented by Alden G. Christianson and Bruce A. Tichenor, from the Federal Water Quality Administration's Pacific Northwest Water Laboratory, at hearings of the Joint Committee on Atomic Energy. It shows that the additional costs incurred by closed cycle cooling are not nearly as high as might be imagined. On the average, around one percent would be added to the electric bill.

TABLE 5: PERCENT COST INCREASE FOR
AVERAGE U.S. CONSUMER

Cooling System	Industrial	Commercial	Residential
Once-through Sea Water	0.34%	0.16%	0.14%
Cooling Pond	0.94%	0.43%	0.39%
Wet Mechanical Draft Cooling Tower	3.17%	1.41%	1.28%
Wet Natural Draft Cooling Tower	1.48%	0.68%	0.62%

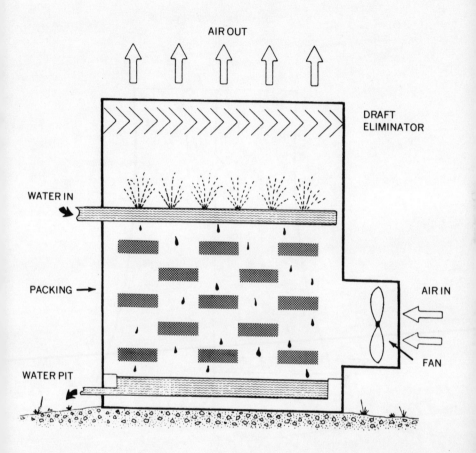

Mechanical forced draft cooling tower

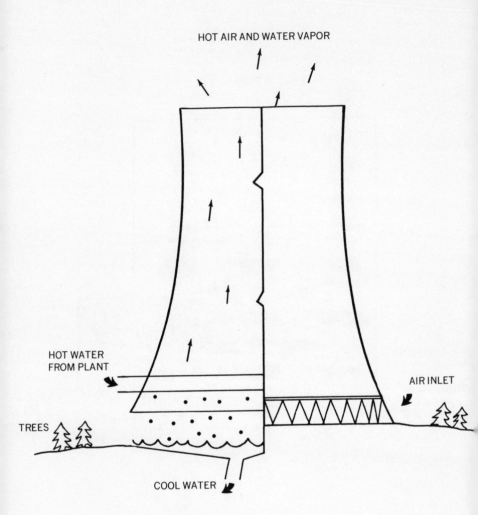

Hyperbolic natural draft cooling tower

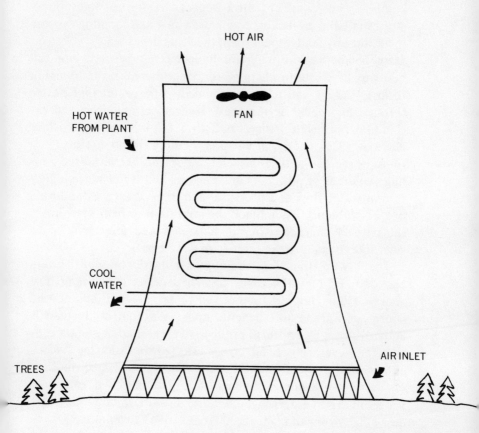

Dry cooling tower

The hyperbolic structures of the newer cooling towers may be pleasing when compared to the aesthetics of an industrial complex, but they are always enormous, sometimes thirty stories tall and a block in diameter, a vast and looming eyesore in almost any landscape, except the most degraded.

Dam boomerangs. Why are hydroelectric projects *not* the best way of providing clean power, since there is no combustion to dirty the air and nothing is added to the water that passes through hydroelectric turbines? Hydroelectric power generation may not result in direct pollution, but it is not ecologically clean at all. As noted in Chapter 1, there simply are no locations where the natural flow of water can be harnessed into huge volumes of power. Dams must be built to produce a high rate of water flow and pressure, and dams create a Pandora's box of problems. They block the migration of fish. They upset the natural characteristics of a stream and may bring considerable changes to the ecology of a river basin.

The Aswan High Dam in Egypt is a classic, but not the only case of an ecological boomerang in hydroelectric planning. The Aswan High Dam was conceived to bring Egyptians power, enormous agricultural benefits and flood control. Instead it actually upset agricultural productivity, resulted in greater erosion than ever before, adversely affected an estuarine fishery and created a major health hazard. The dam stopped the flow of nutrient-bearing sediments that had enriched estuarine waters in the Mediterranean Sea. As a result, the Egyptian sardine catch dropped from 18,000 tons in 1965 to a mere 500 tons in 1968. Delta lands that had been enhanced by loads of silt from upstream were denied natural fertilization and were opened up to attack from the sea, resulting in erosion. Seasonal flooding had always flushed away the soil salts that naturally accumulate along waterways. However, in the stabilized waters produced by the dam, these salts built up and the saline content of the delta lands increased disastrously.

The seasonal flooding of the river had also flushed away the snails that carry the vectors of a debilitating variety of diseases, especially schistosomiasis. But in the standing waters of the lake behind the dam and in the perennially irrigated lands below it, the snails could thrive year round. Schistosomiasis increased phenomenally. Whatever the agricultural benefits that might have derived from the irrigation projects below the dam, they have been more than counteracted by the debilitation of the farmers who were to benefit. Indeed, often as a result of such dam projects as well as other irrigation schemes, schistosomiasis has now become the most serious disease throughout the tropics, and the World Health Organization considers it the prime health matter slowing development in the underdeveloped nations.

Water weeds was another effect noted with dismay only a few short years after the Aswan High Dam was built. These grew at an explosive rate in the new lake and gave up so much moisture through transpiration that the capacity of the lake to drive the hydroelectric turbines in the dam has been threatened.

In the United States, dams have had a more subtle, but often as deleterious, effect on the environment. (One need not fear an outbreak of schistosomiasis in the U.S. because the snails for transmitting it do not and, apparently, can not live here.) Dams have shaped patterns of American agriculture and settlement, particularly in the Southwest and southern California. Quite often they have spoiled wilderness areas. They have encouraged growth in the desert while diverting water from areas that had a natural environmental capacity for a stable population. They have promoted a confident settlement of flood plains without supplying the total flood control promised, with the result that billions of dollars have been lost in the occasional but inevitable floods of our large rivers. Controversies over dams, such as the proposed Salem Church Dam near Fredericksburg, continue to stir up conservationists. A dam may originally be proposed for flood control, with added benefits in the production of hydroelectric energy. As conservationists attack, these two justifications become less important in the engineers' reckoning, replaced by "needs" for water storage or a means by which rivers can periodically be flushed of pollutants or for recreation. Dams continue to be built, but rarely, at the present, for power.

Effects on Air

Electric plants are major polluters of the air. In terms of emissions volume, they are surpassed only by the automobile and all other industries combined. In 1968, power plants emitted 14.4 million tons of sulfur oxides, nearly half the nationwide total; 3.3 million tons of oxides of nitrogen, about one-third the nationwide total; and 3 million tons of particulates, which is about ten percent of the national total. If combustion processes are not cleaned up, these figures would rise by the year 2000 to 49.7 million tons, 10.2 million tons, and 10.2 million tons, respectively.

The adverse effects of sulfur oxides, oxides of nitrogen and particulates—not to mention other harmful air properties—have been well documented by now. It is also well known that the safety levels for these pollutants (the arbitrary limits established through air quality hearings and in accordance with advice from health officials) are exceeded in virtually every large metropolitan area—by as much as three- or fourfold in cities like New York, Chicago and Los Angeles.

Sulfur and nitrogen.   Of the 14.4 million tons of sulfur oxides from utilities in 1968, coal-fired plants produced 13.3 million tons. A short-term solution has been to convert to oil as a fuel, since it contains less sulfur. Energy economists, the Federal Power Commission and others have pointed out that there is an ample supply of low sulfur coal (.7 to 1.0 percent sulfur compared to the typical content of 3 to 4 percent) in the U.S., but that it is located mainly west of the Mississippi River. Supplies in the east are ample to enable coal-burning plants to go a long way towards meeting air quality standards, but the low sulfur coal in eastern coal fields is in high demand by foreign and domestic metallurgical industries making it more expensive. Its two or three dollars extra cost per ton makes it an unlikely or, at least, uneconomic source of fuel for electric plants.

Driven by the need to meet federal air quality standards, fossil-fuel plants have turned to techniques for desulfurizing their fuel. But desulfurization is expensive. In 1970, the cost of reducing the sulfur content in oil from 2.5 percent to .5 percent ranged from fifty to seventy cents per barrel. This is more than twenty percent of the price of a barrel. At the same time, it cost fifty to seventy-five cents per ton of coal to reduce the sulfur content from 3.0 to 1.5 percent. Scrubbing devices in combustion stacks are even more costly, ranging from two to three dollars to remove ninety percent of the sulfur oxides in a ton of coal.

The 1970 Air Quality Act has resulted in such stiff standards on sulfur oxides, particulates and oxides of nitrogen that power plants surely will have to burn cleaner fuels as well as install devices to control and clean the emissions from combustion furnaces. By July 1, 1972, the states must submit air quality programs for approval by the federal government and they must comply with these standards by July 1, 1975. As of this writing, in mid-1971, power company officials were anxious, and well they might be. *New York Times* correspondent E.C. Kenworthy reported in a special survey, April 25, 1971, that power companies had been slow and reluctant to develop a technology to meet new air quality standards, particularly regarding sulfur oxides emissions. Virtually nothing has been done about developing control techniques for oxides of nitrogen, a key contributor to ozone concentrations which in turn make smog. Stack controls and other ways of recovering sulfur were primitive and costly.

The Tennessee Valley Authority has led the way in experimenting with techniques to control sulfur oxide emissions. Dry limestone has been injected in furnaces along with coal to react with sulfur oxides in such a way that the combination can be trapped by electrostatic precipators. This process has not proven particularly expensive, but it results in an enormous volume of solid wastes that make the process difficult and inefficient except in rural areas. Moreover, it only reduces sulfur oxides twenty to thirty percent. A wet limestone slurry process is more promising, reducing sulfur oxides up to ninety percent. So far, however, this method has encountered technical difficulties and it also results in a waste disposal problem. *Even so, such a method, say energy economists, would cost no more than thirty dollars a kilowatt,* thus adding about eleven dollars a year to the average household electric bill, not an exorbitant fee for cleaner air.

Fly ash. In 1969, the utilities industry spent more than twice as much on advertising ($90 million) as on research and development ($40 million). In neither case have the expenditures been effective: both their images and their emissions still need a lot of cleaning up. The electrostatic precipitators, mentioned in connection with sulfur oxides, are presently a feasible means of reducing at least one pollutant—particulates, or fly ash. If such devices were installed nationwide, annual fly ash emissions would be cut down from 5.6 million tons to less than 80,000 tons. The trouble is that the average coal plant sends up so much soot that even controls to cope with ninety percent of it allow a great deal to escape. A Washington energy consultant, Wilson Clark, found that a coal-fired plant in Nevada released one ton of fly ash per hour even while using a ninety-seven percent efficient electrostatic precipitator.

Some power plants have used high stacks, over 1,000 feet tall, in an attempt to disperse particulates further afield. These measures, of course, are futile for the long term. The earth's atmospheric blanket will only get thicker, and the overhead haze that afflicts so many regions will continue to shut out more sunlight. And the particulates will continue to get into people's respiratory systems, aggravating bronchial and respiratory conditions and heart disease and, as increasing evidence shows, contributing to cancer. The power companies quite simply are going to have to spend a lot more than the one percent of their annual budgets that they have been investing recently in environmental technology.

Trading off in the Southwest. A dramatic case study of the atmospheric effects of power combustion is provided by a controversy that has embroiled environmentalists and power officials as well as impoverished Indian tribes in the southwestern United States. The battle also poses basic questions in terms of which environmental evil might be traded for another evil. Ironically, the debate has occurred essentially because conservationists fought successfully in the 1960s to prevent the construction of massive hydroelectric facilities in the Grand Canyon. They won a well-deserved victory to stop two dams which would have flooded large sections of the Grand Canyon, destroying natural, geologic and scenic monuments. As David Brower's Sierra Club howled, it would have been like flooding the Sistine Chapel.

But, from an environmental standpoint, it now seems that the alternatives were not much better. Shortly after the defeat of the Grand Canyon dams, some twenty-three utilities formed a consortium and planned, in a first phase, to build six giant plants that would generate 12,000 megawatts of electricity, enough for nine million people. The beneficiaries would include such settlements as Los Angeles, Phoenix, Las Vegas, Albuquerque and Tucson, cities whose air quality problems would not permit the construction of cheap power facilities in their own immediate environs. These six plants were not designed with today's environmental considerations in mind. They could conveniently burn dirty coal that was strip mined nearby, sending electricity far and wide via ugly transmission lines that would scar only the arid desert. Little thought was given to the immemorial concerns and rights of the Indians who live on these desert lands, but that is nothing new. They have never been properly respected. For years and years, the Interior Department, which, among other tasks, acts as the Indians' trustee, has been promoting projects that abuse Indian water, timber, mineral and grazing rights.

By mid-1971, two of the six plants were operating. One of them, the 2.1 million kilowatt Four Corners plant, located near the intersection of Arizona, New Mexico, Colorado and Utah, generally uses up 22,000 tons of strip-mined coal and belches out 350 tons of soot and ash per day—twice the generally particulate load of New York city and nearly three times that of Los Angeles. *The Washington Post*'s Leroy Aarons reported that particulate and sulfur oxide controls at Four Corners and the other five plants, were they all to be installed, would still allow the daily escape of several hundred tons of fly ash emissions and 2,000 tons of sulfur oxides. The Four Corners area is no longer famous for its pristine, clean air.

The water consumption of these plants is fantastic. Four

Corners uses 11 billion gallons a day. The Mojave plant in Nevada, the second facility in operation, gets its coal from Black Mesa, a distance of 275 miles. The coal is pumped through pipes in a slurry of water at a rate of 2,000 gallons a minute. All this is happening in a water-starved region. Nobody has yet shown what the effect will be on deep aquifers that now support the drinking and agricultural needs of the Indian tribes in this region and others who need the water for life support.

There is at least one obvious conflict of interest in the consortium plan. Tbe Bureau of Reclamation is to receive twenty-four percent of the power from one plant, just to pump water to the Central Arizona project, benefiting Phoenix and Tucson.

And yet, is it not the job of the government to protect the interests of the Indians? Since water and fuel come from government or Indian lands, Secretary of Interior Rogers Morton used his power in the spring of 1971 to declare a one-year moratorium on future power plant construction in the Southwest. However, his edict only applied to the sixth facility which is not yet under construction—an enormous five million kilowatt plant planned for Kaiparowits, Utah, which will use billions of gallons of water daily from Lake Powell and 15 million tons of coal annually. And in the year during which the government, state public service commissions and the utilities reassess the impact of the other five plants (the two operating and three presently being built), it appears doubtful that much can be accomplished beyond demanding basic environmental controls in the plants. It would seem too late to plan for new locations or for alternative methods of power generation.

The Indians have not lost hope. Members of the Hopi tribe have brought suit against the Peabody Coal Co., claiming that this producer had obtained the right to strip-mine coal from the Black Mesa from a tribal government that was unrepresentative and illegally constituted. And a Navajo group has sued the Department of Health, Education and Welfare for failing to protect the Indians from the effects of air pollution from the Four Corners plant. The Indians have been joined in the suits by national conservation organizations who have returned to the "glories-of-Rome" analogy that succeeded in the case of the Grand Canyon. The headline of a full-page ad in national newspapers in 1971, sponsored by the Sierra Club, Friends of the Earth, and others intones, ". . . Like Ripping Apart St. Peters, In Order to Sell the Marble."

The Arizona Public Service Commission noted that scrubbing devices costing $14 million would reduce the Four Corners air pollution ninety-nine percent. But as the summer of 1971 ended, a plume of smoke kept right on drifting downwind from Four Corners, often visible as far away as 215 miles.

Oil: Spills, Leaks, Blowouts

Energy policy decisions are complex and far-reaching. They are embedded in domestic and international political consider-ations. In recent years, notably since the wreck of the Torrey Canyon in 1967 which resulted in the spillage of 117,000 tons of oil in the English Channel, some of the most publicized and most upsetting environmental crises have been oil spills. These have resulted from offshore drilling in the Gulf of Mex-ico and Santa Barbara Channel, from collisions, groundings and other mishaps in the transportation of oil at sea and from willful dumping or pumping of bilges.

Among other things, at the root of this problem is the Oil Import Program and other protectionist measures that have resulted from the enormous influence and power of the U.S. oil energy establishment. For example, while the Mandatory Oil Import Quota was established in 1959, solely on the grounds of national security, to encourage domestic oil exploration, it has done quite the opposite. The major oil companies have indulged in extremely profitable bargaining among themselves for import quota "tickets." The huge volume of oil that has been imported and refined in the U.S. has almost entirely gone into gasoline and other light distillates. At present, only six percent of each barrel is, on the average, left as residual oil of the type burned by electric plants. Because oil producers have been able to rig their own markets—in effect, to control demand and supply—it has not been profitable to sell fuel oil in volume. Both the No. 2 home heating oil subject to quotas and Bunker C oil that is used by power companies are exempted from the quota in the northeastern district. The oil companies, however, have recently sought permission to import an increased volume of oil on the grounds that air quality standards have required the refining of low and sulfur fuel. So far, nothing has developed to contradict the snide observation that the oil companies are talking about low-sulfur fuel as an excuse to import more crude stock for conversion into profitable items like gasoline.

Meanwhile, as a result of this kind of operation and other considerations, there is an enormous volume of oil being moved by ships at sea. According to the Woods Hole Oceanographic Institute at least 5 million tons of the oil, and possibly twice that, is dumped or spilled into the sea each year. The oceans are contaminated mainly along the coastal shelf near the harbors and estuaries where seventy percent of the world's commercial fish are produced or nurtured.

In an article in the March, 1971, issue of *Environment,* four scientists from the Woods Hole Oceanographic Institute presented research indicating that day-to-day spills of oil are beginning to have a discernible and adverse influence on the aquatic food chain. All hydrocarbons do not evaporate; some settle on the bottom in toxic concentrations. Small marine organisms are poisoned and the tissues of larger fish as well as shellfish accumulate oil traces that are believed to produce carcinogenic effects higher up in the food chain.

Since sixty percent of the world's oil production is transported by ships, spills at sea pose a major hazard. And now vessels of 370,000 deadweight tons, three times the size of the ill-fated Torrey Canyon, are presently being built to haul oil.

Oil companies, prodded by government, insurance companies and self-interest, are seeking ways to control spills and to clean them up when they do occur. In general, the cleanup techniques are very crude. Dispersants sink to the bottom or drive the hydrocarbons to the bottom resulting in ecological damage. Booms, scoops, containment devices—all are being tried but they rarely make it to the scene of a spill in time to prevent considerable pollution damage, and so far they have proved largely inadequate in any kind of heavy wave action.

World offshore oil production is another hazard. Now totalling 6.5 million barrels a day, offshore yields are quite likely going to quadruple in the next decade. Offshore mineral deposits are also believed likely to hold the natural gas reserves so badly needed for clean combustion. In 1969 and 1970, U.S. offshore facilities erupted oil in both the Santa Barbara Channel and the Gulf of Mexico. Both disasters resulted from human negligence or lack of precaution. Since then, drilling has continued in both offshore areas, although under increased scrutiny by federal officials. This country, as yet, has no firm policy or priorities with respect to offshore oil. Because more spills cannot be entirely avoided, we are going to have to decide what is the best use of the continental shelf—to produce food or fuels.

The movement or handling of oil at sea is not the only oil transportation problem. The land environment must also be considered, and a classic case where land and sea considerations come into conflict is in Alaska. Under the Artic north slope, there are said to be billions of barrels of oil. The question is how to get it to the populous, urban regions of the U.S. without damaging the environment. At the moment, it does not seem feasible to ship the oil from Prudhoe Bay to eastern ports via the Northwest Passage because of the dangers of ice along this route. And pumping the oil via a 789-mile pipeline to the Port of Valdez, from where it would be shipped to the West Coast, also is fraught with a variety of environmental dangers that had not been resolved by the end of the summer of 1971. Much of the pipe would go through permafrost. Technology has not yet provided for construction of a pipeline in this sort of ground that will not leave great, lasting scars. No one knows what to do when warm oil moving through a pipe melts the frozen spongy ground that supports that pipe. A pipeline leak would loose millions of gallons of oil before it could be checked, threatening a great, unspoiled wilderness and wildlife watershed. Since most of the planned pipeline route is on federal land, and most of this land involves native Indian claims, the federal government's permission is necessary before a pipe can be constructed or major access routes built. By mid-1971, Interior Secretary Rogers Morton had delayed a decision regarding federal lands. Court action is certain in any event and Morton's decision, whenever it comes, is likely to trigger a congressional inquiry.

The Factors of Land Use

Obviously, the ill effects on air and water from generating electricity are ultimately connected to the overall matter of land use. A plant using "once-through" cooling techniques, for example, requires an ample source of water, preferably one which is nearby. We have seen how the utilities in the Southwest went ahead with a coal-fired power complex on the basis that the smallest number of people—and, in their view, the least important people—would be affected by the resulting pollution.

There are, however, an infinite number of land-use considerations in addition to those connected with the pollution factors we have discussed so far. The most salient, though often overlooked, of these land-use problems are the hazards of mining fuel, power transmission, rights-of-way and misplaced priorities with respect to site location.

Side effects of mining. The mining of coal—both underground and by open-pit and strip methods—has resulted in an untold devastation of land and lives. It is one of the prices of energy production. In the Appalachian region alone, over 10,000 miles of waterways have been severely polluted as the result of acid wastes draining from mining operations that have been abandoned or that are still in use. In some twenty-six states, bulldozers, enormous stripping machines and augur drills five feet in diameter are devouring seams of well over 100 billion tons of coal. Once the land has been stripped and devastated, it is left to erode. Federal and state laws presently do not force mining companies to do nearly enough to prevent such destruction or to reclaim the land they strip.

Strip mining presently accounts for forty percent of U.S. coal production. In 1968, when this method accounted for thirty-four percent, over 201 million tons of coal were gouged from the surface of the land. According to the U.S. Geological Survey, no more and probably less than one-third of the 3,000 square miles of the U.S. that have been strip mined has been reclaimed or made into reusable land. (Much of the reclamation that *is* done is merely cosmetic, preventing further erosion but not making the land productive again.) And yet Geological Survey papers point out that far less than one-twentieth of the surface coal in this country has been tapped. Reclaiming devastated land to a satisfactory degree is expensive, ranging from three hundred to three thousand dollars an acre, depending on the characteristics of the terrain. There are several bills pending in the U.S. Congress that would allow strip mining only under strictly regulated conditions and environmental standards prescribing reclamation. As this book was written, none had been passed and only West Virginia had enacted a truly tough bill on the subject. It banned strip mining in twenty-two counties for two years, pending a study of better techniques, and doubled the bond companies must pay in order to ensure that they will conduct a reclamation program.

Underground mining is not free from environmental hazards either. Worse, from the standpoint of health and occupational safety, *it is the most dangerous industry in the U.S.* Respiratory sickness and pneumoconiosis—the so-called "black-lung" disease—have afflicted many thousands of coal miners. Wilson Clark, the Washington consultant cited earlier, correctly points out that "these social costs must be taken into account in a comparison of the role of coal production in the energy industries."

Two years ago, in a draft of a report entitled "Environmental Effects of Underground Mining and of Mineral Processing," prepared for the Bureau of Mines, the extraordinary long-term effects of underground mining were presented in horrifying detail. Some two million acres of land have subsided or caved in as a result of underground excavations, uncontrolled fires have been burning for years in these mines, and refuse tailings have been left to drain away near countless mining communities. The town of Scranton, Pennsylvania, for example, is seriously threatened by underground subsidence, although most collapses from past mining activities occur in rural regions. Even so, acid drainage from mines has damaged crops and contaminated water supplies. The Bureau of Mines report, which was given no publicity at all until people's advocate Ralph Nader brought attention to it, said that little or nothing was being done to stabilize past damage from underground mining and that, if the situation were allowed to continue unchecked, another 2.5 million acres of land would be seriously degraded by the year 2000.

Rights-of-way. Transmitting power and fuel for power is a major aspect of the energy crisis that goes largely unnoticed except by those individual property owners and conservation organizations who are concerned about the aesthetic and ecological effects on land wrought by pipelines and high voltage wires.

We have mentioned the well-published hazards connected with the Trans-Alaska Pipeline that would bring oil from Prudhoe Bay to Valdez or, if any alternative route is decided upon, from Prudhoe Bay through the Arctic Wildlife Refuge into Canada and the continental United States. Already in place and raising serious questions are more than one million miles of underground pipelines carrying natural gas from the Southwest. While gas company officials hold that pipelines are thick enough to withstand a good deal of shock, federal officials are troubled about the dangers of underground explosions. Yet to date, there has been little official assessment of the hazards posed by these pipelines and the environmental safeguards that may or may not be needed. Numerous leaks and some big explosions have been reported in recent years, and it is certain that public fears will be voiced at an increasing rate as more land is condemned for pipeline rights-of-way.

An Office of Science and Technology report (see Bibliography) entitled *Electric Power and the Environment* in August,

1970, noted that "literally millions of acres of rights-of-way land would be required in the next two decades for the growth of utilities and their tremendous needs for transmission lines along with the expansion of highways, interstate gas lines, water supply lines, etc. It is imperative," the report continued, "that land be used more efficiently for all competing demands." To date, government planners at all levels have failed to get a handle on this problem. Already high voltage transmission lines, taking power from generating plants to distribution substations, cover more than three hundred thousand miles of the U.S. landscape. Averaging one hundred and ten feet wide, the rights-of-way for these lines use up about four million acres. At present, it is not economically feasible, nor has the technology been perfected, to put high voltage lines underground, except in tunnels which are used for other conduits. In addition, electric and gas utilities, with few exceptions, have not gotten together to develop common transmission corridors.

Citizen groups have in recent years been tremendously vocal and in some cases successful in protesting the blight caused by transmission lines. In the future, as power plants are located away from metropolitan areas in order to minimize air and water pollution, there will have to be many more transmission corridors. By 1990, it is estimated another three million acres will be so taken up if present trends go unremedied.

Siting. This entire chapter has been concerned indirectly with characteristics influencing the location of power plants and transmitting facilities. The sheer costs of land and the desirability of that land for recreation areas parks or residential developments pose a host of problems that energy policy planners are only beginning to perceive. The plants now on the drawing boards will be much larger than past facilities, and environmental controls—cooling ponds and so forth—will require a considerable amount of additional land. On the average, a new coal plant will take up to 1,200 acres; a nuclear plant up to 400 acres, a gas turbine plant up to 200 acres and an oil-fired plant up to 350 acres.

A power plant must be located with efficient and economic

access to fuel supplies. Steam plants need water for cooling. More often than not, utilities are in competition with heavy industries for plant sites, and the growing scarcity of undeveloped waterfront has created a variety of new environmental concerns regarding shoreline property. For example, the oil industry seeks new deep-water ports to accommodate deep-drafted supertankers where refineries also can be built to produce low-sulfur fuel. Power plants would be built near these oil complexes. Recreation colonists also want this land for shorefront cottages, marinas and beaches.

A dramatic instance of just this kind of conflict took place in Delaware in June, 1971. Led by the state's governor, the legislature passed a bill forbidding further industrial development of Delaware Bay, requiring that what remains of that highly industrialized shoreline be kept for recreation and conservation. This action was taken in spite of pressure from industry. The federal government—both the Department of the Treasury and the Department of Commerce—strongly advised the state that the continued industrial development of the Bay and its use as one of the few remaining deep-water ports on the East Coast were essential to the world trade position of the country as a whole.

Up to the present, planning by utilities has been shortsighted and secretive. It is understandable that electric companies do not want to drive up the price of land by announcing long in advance where they plan to build. Neither do they want opposition groups to have time to organize for public hearings or even litigation. However, the time has come for comprehensive, farsighted land-use planning on the part of the energy industry. Otherwise, as will be seen in the following chapter, their costs may go even higher and severe power shortages may also result.

Nuclear Power

Electrical energy generated in nuclear plants is considered by many to be the best solution to the power needs of the United States. Among other things, nuclear power avoids several of the environmental liabilities mentioned so far in this chapter: primarily, it avoids the forms of air pollution that fossil fuel plants create.

There are currently twenty-one nuclear power plants operating in the United States, and some ninety-three under construction or in the planning stage. By 2000, the Atomic Energy Commission forsees 950 plants in operation. The "nukes," as they are called, are unquestionably *here*—perhaps to stay. But with them comes a host of new questions and the answers are far from clear.

First of all, how do the nukes work? Basically they work in the same way as other plants: they heat up water to make steam to drive a generator. In a typical, pressurized water nuclear plant, the reactor core produces heat which is transferred to water sealed in the reactor. Under tremendous pressure, this super-hot water does not turn to steam. Instead, it is pumped to a boiler where it gives off its heat to other water already in the boiler and returns to the reactor to pick up more heat. Meanwhile the water that was heated in the boiler becomes steam which turns a turbine which drives the generator. The steam reverts to water in a condenser which is itself cooled by yet another water supply pumped in from the ocean, a river, or a cooling pond or cooling tower (see p. 17-19).

There was a time, over a decade ago, when a great many people feared that the new part of this largely familiar system—that is, the nuclear reactor—entailed the dangers of an atomic explosion. Visions of A-bomb mushroom clouds rising over the nation's cities from accidents in its own power plants led many people to oppose even the thought of using nuclear power for electricity. The Atomic Energy Commission spent a good deal of time explaining, rightly, that no such danger exists. A nuclear reactor simply works on a different principle. But it does entail a variety of other hazards and environmental problems. However, the AEC, the nuclear industry, and the scientists and administrators and publicists connected with nuclear power have been far less than candid in discussing the degree of the dangers and unknowns involved in the production of power in nuclear plants. Five years ago, an assistant to one of the members of Congress most interested in the scientific aspects of nuclear power told one of the authors of this book that there was no way to get a debate going, in Congressional hearings, on the subject because "all the experts on the subject work for the industry." The AEC is almost alone in its roles as both a promoter *and* regulator of atomic energy and, until very recently, the AEC has been almost immune from sharp-penciled overseeing from Congress.

What is there to oversee? What, if any, are the hazards of nuclear power? Aside from the environmental tradeoffs connected with the use of water and land which have already been discussed, nuclear energy's environmental—thus ultimately human—hazards fall into three categories: the "normal" operating leakages of radioactive materials into the air and water, the danger of industrial accident in nuclear plants, and the disposal of used "hot" waste material from the reactor. All three categories of problems have recently and vigorously been raised and, to an extent, debated. The answers are by no means clear, nor are the facts, largely because of the industry's desire to play it close to the chest. Until recently, and even now in many cases, critics and questioners have been treated with condescension as to their scientific qualifications, or with the kind of acid disdain with which all Cassandras such as Rachel Carson have traditionally been met. Few Cassandras in history, it should be emphasized, have been altogether correct, but the questions that have been raised about nuclear power are serious ones and they should certainly be discussed openly and candidly.

Radiation. Mankind has evolved in an environment in which he has always been exposed to a certain amount of natural background radiation from rocks and space. The annual amount is equivalent to a dental X-ray. There is a certain amount of leakage of radioactivity from nuclear power plants into the air and the coolant water during the normal operation of a nuclear plant. The industry says that a person living right beside a nuclear plant will receive about one percent more radiation annually than he would from natural radiation. Is that safe?

What is clear from all of the literature, reports, debates, and experiments to date, is that no one really knows yet what is safe either for humans or for aquatic food chains. The AEC has said that of all those people who live downwind from a nuclear plant only one person every ten years could die from radiation. If they are right, this is certainly an improvement over the probable number of deaths resulting each year from air pollution by fossil fuel plants.

However, these figures have been disputed. Two scientists, John Gofman and Arthur Tamplin, both from the Lawrence Radiation Laboratory in Livermore, California, have said that 60,000 additional deaths from cancer per year could occur from nuclear plants if radiation pollution for those plants reached the AEC's present permissible levels. Other scientists have made equally alarming, though different, estimates, and all of these critics have been dismissed as alarmists, if not paranoids.

The estimated dose from a nuclear power plant—some one percent per year of background radiation—is well below the present "maximum permissible dose" set by the National Council on Radiation Protection and Measurement. Safety devices are being developed to reduce these emissions even further and the AEC in 1971 revised the maximum permissible dose downwards a hundredfold. This would seem to be safe enough but biologists have not had the time to discover what a continuous additional percentage of radiation, however slight, will do to human populations. It would seem wise to be wary—even of the experts.

Radioactive wastes.   A nuclear reactor produces some two hundred radioactive isotopes. Some of the isotopes, such as iodine 131, decay in a few days; others, like uranium 238 and plutonium 239, coninue to be radioactive for thousands of years. Some of a plant's radioactive material leaks into the air or the coolant water; most is held as waste deposits.

Where are the waste products of nuclear plants taken? What happens to them then? Hundreds of thousands of gallons of radioactive liquids are injected into the ground; others, which are so hot that they keep boiling for years, are kept by the AEC

in giant tanks. These tanks are stored in facilities in
Washington, South Carolina, Idaho and Illinois. The AEC
intends to solidify these wastes after they have cooled and to
store them in abandoned salt mines. Citizens of Kansas, the
state that has been selected for this new sort of warehousing,
have become deeply concerned, and by mid-summer of 1971
Senator Robert Dole, who is a Kansas senator as well as
National Republican Committee Chairman, had called for a
complete review of the technology of storing such materials.

The AEC and the nuclear industry may well be the most
safety conscious organizations in the world, even their critics
make this claim. Enormous care and the most elaborate pre-
cautions have been and are being taken. Yet, it is also perfectly
clear that nothing like this has ever been attempted before.
The industry assures us that they have—or will develop—
the technology to cope.

Accidents.   In October of 1966, the Enrico Fermi nuclear
plant near Detroit embarked on, what is called by reactor engineers, a "grand excursion." It did not complete the trip.
Had it done so, according to a University of Michigan report,
over 100,000 people would have been killed, the city would
have had to be evacuated, and an agricultural quarantine might
have been necessary over a vast area of the Midwest.

A "grand excursion" is a term used to describe a runaway
reactor, and one consequence of such an event that engineers
have planned for is a "melt-down." If the reactor were to lose
its coolant water through some kind of rupture in the cooling
system, the reactor would heat up rapidly. But a back-up
coolant system (the emergency core coolant system) would
then go into operation and keep the reactor under control.

If the emergency coolant system failed, the temperature in
the fuel rods in the reactor would go from their normal 600
degrees Fahrenheit to over 3,000 degrees in a minute or less.
This is a higher temperature than the container for the fuel rods
can withstand and there would follow a complete melt-down of
the reactor. Tons of molten metal would fall to the bottom of
the reactor vessel through the concrete and would proceed on
what nuclear engineers call the "Chinese syndrome," meaning

that China would be the direction in which the hot metal would be heading—by the most direct route. There might finally be steam and gas explosions that would scatter radioactive material to the winds.

In March, 1971, research on emergency core cooling systems led AEC scientists to the conclusion that they might not work. They are now part of the design of some sixty plants scheduled to go into operation in the next decade. The AEC announced that it would begin extensive testing of these systems in their Idaho research station. All the previous testing has been mathematical. The AEC has also delayed their installation in several plants now under construction, thus delaying the completion of the plants altogether. But for several years, there have been public assurances that there was nothing wrong, from an engineering standpoint, with nuclear power plants.

Here, then, is the dilemma. Public safety is publicly assured: it has to be assured or the public will howl. Serious men do their best to assure *in actuality* the public safety, yet their efforts are found, often by themselves, to be lacking. These same serious men seek larger budgets for research and development in the safety area and are turned down. Meanwhile, if *you* question the safety of these plants, you are asked to leave such matters to the experts.

In July, 1971, *Science* magazine quoted an outspoken but anonymous nuclear safety expert in the AEC as saying, "We think we can set boundary conditions, so no matter how a reactor goes we are quite sure it's safe. But I find having to work this way intellectually less satisfying . . . I prefer to *know*, in a quantifiable way, what the limits of safety are."

The AEC meets NEPA

On July 23, 1971, a U.S. Court of Appeals in the District of Columbia issued a decision which took the AEC to task for its failure to comply with the requirements of the National Environmental Protection Act of 1970. Specifically, the issue concerned the Calvert Cliffs reactor, under construction in Maryland on Cheasapeake Bay, but its effects will have ramifications throughout the industry, possibly holding up or temporarily closing down some ninety-one reactors under construction or completed since passage of the act.

The court criticized the AEC for simply following other agencies' guidelines, such as federal or state water pollution laws, and not making its own, for excluding outsiders from raising environmental questions, for excluding many environmental factors altogether, and for not taking each reactor's licensing on a case by case basis, as the act requires.

When the commission discussed the national power crisis as a reason for trying to avoid what it considered "unreasonable delays," the court answered, in what may become an environmentalists' motto, "The spectre of the national power crisis must not be used to create a blackout of environmental considerations."

Thus chastened in some of the strongest language yet used by a court involved in interpreting NEPA, the AEC returned to the drawing boards to produce its own environmental guidelines, as requested, and announced that it would not appeal the District Court's decision. In August, under its new chief, Dr. James R. Schesinger, an economist and a reported birdwatcher, the AEC announced a new policy of openness. Information would, henceforth, be more freely available and environmentalists would be taken more seriously.

Trading

The environmental liabilities of generating electricity are beginning to be known. Many can already be measured. Many can certainly be dealt with. Many, however, are not known and are a long way from being measured.

There *is* no simple answer. Even the most environmentally acute students and organizations concerned with power, admit that no one existing mode is the right way, or the wrong way. It depends on the individual circumstances. It is too simple to say, for example, that using nuclear generation in place of the conventional modes is to trade a number of known evils for some benefits and a host of unknown evils. It is more complicated than that.

Some of the complications can best be seen by observing how

one utility has tried to cope with the dilemma of power. The next chapter takes a look at Consolidated Edison of New York, a utility that knows what it looks like on the edge of the precipice.

CHAPTER 3

CON ED:
AN ECOLOGICAL
PERSPECTIVE

July 17, 1969 was a bad day for Consolidated Edison Company of New York, the utility that ranks by most yardsticks as the world's largest with operating revenues over $1 billion, 4.1 million customers and assets approaching $5 billion. The day dawned clear, hot and humid—the kind of torrid weather that makes people lunge for their air conditioners. A peak load of 7,200 megawatts had been forecasted. It was going to be a hot day throughout the Northeast, and Con Ed knew that it could not count on getting additional power from outside power companies. Officials at the utility knew they would not be able to muster up more than 7,403 megawatts, certainly not enough to maintain a safe margin of reserve against the twin possibilities of even higher than expected demands and an equipment failure. By 12:45 that afternoon, Con Ed's generators were severely strained, putting out over 7,000 megawatts of power, and it was necessary to resort to one of many power-saving alternatives: the utility reduced voltage by three percent. Even so, and with an additional 396 megawatts of imported power, Con Ed's load peaked at 4:00 P.M. to 7,292 megawatts. Shortly thereafter, the load began to decline slightly, but the power exporters began to want some of their electricity back, and a reserve margin still was needed, so Con Ed ordered a five percent voltage reduction.

The next day was even worse. The first real summer test had taken its toll. The 400-megawatt Ravenswood No. 2 Unit went out of service because of a boiler leak. Just before midnight on the 17th, feedwater leakage at the Arthur Kill Station caused another 340 megawatts to go off the line. Earlier in the evening, a fire at the Hudson Station accounted for a 400-megawatt loss in generating power. And early on the morning of the 18th, the Indian Point Station had a failure that took out 230 megawatts. All told, as the thermometer rose on July 18th, Con Ed met the heat wave with 1,370 fewer megawatts. *This happened at a time when the utility's peak demand was expected to reach a record of 7,350 megawatts.*

At daybreak, Con Ed officials frantically telephoned their largest customers, pleading for electricity savings, what is known in the language of the power business as "voluntary curtailment of nonessential loads." As New Yorkers were eating breakfast or commuting to work early, the utility appealed by radio, television and newspaper for electrical austerity. All the power Con Ed expected to be able to generate was 6,800 megawatts, about 1,138 megawatts short of what was needed to keep a safe reserve. Maintenance crews that had worked all night restored 384 megawatts. But by 9:17 A.M. it had become necessary to order a three percent voltage reduction. The load was climbing fast, but fortunately the appeals were effective: the peak which was reached at 4:30 P.M. did not exceed 6,938 megawatts.

All that summer, Con Ed was plagued with crises. No sooner would one breakdown be fixed than another generator would stop. About a third of the equipment was forty or more years old and could not take the strain.

As the sun rose August 4, Con Ed had never been in a more precarious position. The No. 3 Allis-Chalmers generator at Ravenswood, known as "Big Allis" for its 1,030 megawatts of power, had broken down on July 31 and was under emergency repairs. Another 770 megawatts were lost in additional failures. The predicted peak load of 6,400 megawatts was less than previous peaks, but Con Ed could only generate 6,450 megawatts. This included imported power in the amount of 1,156 megawatts. By 8:30 that morning, a three percent voltage reduction went into effect. At 9:20 A.M., a five percent reduction was ordered. At 9:27 A.M., a breakdown occurred which took out an additional 82 megawatts, so Con Ed reduced voltage eight per cent. Again, mass public appeals saved the day.

Charles Luce, the relatively new president of Con Ed, was in charge of "saving the day," almost every day it seemed. Luce possessed an exemplary record, particularly as a friend of conservationists. He had come to Con Ed in the spring of 1967 after serving as Under Secretary of the Department of the Interior, second man under Stewart Udall. Despite a leg handicap caused by polio, he had a reputation as a game outdoorsman and as an avid bicyclist. He had come to Con Ed promising to open up the record, to provide the public well in advance with full knowledge of Con Ed's plans and policies and to fight pollution. Immediately, the utility's slogan was changed from "Dig We Must" to "Clean Energy."

But Luce was confronted with problems on all sides. Con Ed had lost the trust of the business community and was having difficulty raising capital. Con Ed's management was tired and gray, and, in some cases, corrupt. The company had certainly been inefficient and, even worse, sometimes hostile and secretive in its dealings with the public. Luce was forced to fight a rear guard action while rebuilding a viable offense in the form of progressive management and planning apparatus. At the time this book was written, he had made little progress, and the game really seemed beyond his control. When Luce took command, Con Ed's major troubles resulted, as they still do, from confrontations with environmentalists—especially in the area of air and water standards.

During the height of the 1969 power crisis, right after New York City had gone through a harrowing series of brownouts, one of the authors interviewed Luce in his office. "Big Allis" had been repaired but nerves were still taut. Looking out his office window to the north, where Big Allis had just begun to operate again, Luce remarked that, "our best hope is to get more public understanding of the growing demands for power and of the fact that any plant we build will have some adverse impact on the environment."

The chronology of Con Ed's troubles regarding environmental concerns is well worth tracing in some detail, because it illustrates the depth, complexity and near hopelessness of the dilemma facing both utilities and the electricity-hungry public. All of the environmental "tradeoffs" are featured; Luce's contention that the environment cannot come off clean, in spite of the utility's cheerful new slogan, is a point of seeming validity. In Con Ed's case, the predicament is compounded by difficult economic and political questions, the best answers to which suggest that a major upheaval will be necessary in the free enterprise system, sooner rather than later, if we are to keep the lights burning.

For our purposes, the chronology begins in 1962 when Con Ed projected demands for power—and ways to provide it—for the next decade. What Luce now calls the "keystone" of the utility's plans to cope with the demand was its proposal to build a two million kilowatt pumped-storage plant at Storm King Mountain, on the Hudson River at Cornwall. The engineering concept was ingenious. It required a reservoir to be built 1,000 feet above the river, just over the top of the mountain. During the off hours, when demands on Con Ed's old steam generators were low, excess electrical energy would be used to pump water up into the reservoir. Then, on a moment's notice, during peak hours when the old system was strained, the reservoir would be poured back to the Hudson driving generator turbines that would send power through transmission wires to New York, fifty miles to the south. From an economic standpoint the proposal was also ideal, because it was technically so simple. But it opened a hornet's nest. Conservationists accurately contended that the project would mar the Hudson Highlands, a scenic gorge which in 1778 had moved Timothy Dwight, an Army chaplain and later first president of Yale, to note that it was "difficult to conceive of anything more solemn or wild than the appearance of these mountains."

The Scenic Hudson Preservation Conference was formed,

the first of several citizen organizations stirred into existence by Con Ed. Scenic Hudson hired excellent lawyers who vigorously and imaginatively fought the Storm King proposal. The pumped-storage project had been counted on to satisfy peak demands for power by 1967. In the summer of 1971, it was being debated in court and could not possibly be built before 1980. Construction estimates had skyrocketed from $162 million to $400 million. Compared to the one million dollars Scenic Hudson had spent to fight the project, Con Ed had spent, by this time, more than $14 million in litigation and modifications of the plan to suit the opposition. Added to this cost were the construction of a 500,000-kilowatt conventional plant on Staten Island and constant repairs and deferred retirement on old generators, all of which were necessary to make up the interim power deficit caused by the Storm King battle.

At the outset of the Storm King hearings, Con Ed officials behaved badly. They were arrogant towards well-meaning conservationists. They glossed over potentially adverse ecological effects that the consumption and release of great volumes of water (six billion gallons a day) would cause in the Hudson, particularly on the schools of spawning striped bass and shad. Then, the utility concealed from the public the fact, which it later admitted, that thermal pollution from the Indian Point nuclear plant fifteen miles south of Storm King had killed millions of fish when it went into operation in 1962.

By 1964, the "new conservation" movement had gathered momentum. The beautification of America, a theme begun by Lady Bird Johnson and carried out by Stewart Udall, had political clout. Democrat Richard Ottinger defeated a Republican incumbent for Congress by basing his campaign in Westchester County and environs largely on his opposition to the Cornwall project. Con Ed made a few concessions. The company agreed to landscape the powerhouse and to bury transmission lines that would have crossed the Hudson River. Con Ed also wooed the town of Cornwall by promising economic benefits, a new water system for the town and cosmetic improvements along the waterfront. The lobbying paid off. On March 10, 1965, the Federal Power Commission approved the plan, saying that "Whatever may be the negative aspects of adding this on Storm King Mountain, on balance we do not believe it outweighs the public interests in the effective utilization of an unusually fine pumped-storage site."

Later that year, on an appeal by the conservationists, the New York Second Court of Appeals ruled that new hearings would have to be held and that the FPC's "renewed proceedings must include as a basic concern the preservation of natural beauty and of national historic shrines, keeping in mind that, in our affluent society, the cost of a project is only one of several factors to be considered."

Since then, Con Ed has agreed to additional aesthetic modifications, the placing of the powerhouse underground and contributions towards a waterfront park. Responding to the court's dictum that alternative sites also should be considered, the FPC suggested moving the project under the State Palisades Park, a mile down-river, but Con Ed had no stomach for the fight that this proposal would surely stir up. Meanwhile, the City of New York joined the battle, on the side of the environmental coalition, by contending that underground facilities at Storm King would seriously endanger an aqueduct one hundred feet below that carried vital water supplies to the city from the Catskill Mountains. When the FPC ruled again, on August 23, 1970, that Cornwall could at last be built, the opposition took the whole matter back to court. (As this book went to press, the U.S. Court of Appeals, Second Circuit, ruled in favor of Con Ed and the opposition's only hope was to have the Cornwall proposal argued in the U.S. Supreme Court.) Meanwhile, on August 18, 1971, New York State Commissioner of Environmental Conservation, Henry L. Diamond, rather lamely backed the FPC by certifying Storm King as being environmentally sound. If the $234 million project were found to violate water quality standards, it would be halted immediately, said Diamond, thus offering a sop to Storm King opponents that would seem impossible to apply later on and that takes the burden of proof off the backs of both the state and Con Ed.

At the beginning of the Storm King battle, conservationists pointed out that Con Ed would obtain considerable amounts of future power from nuclear plants at Indian Point, from gas turbines and through contracts with other utilities. As the Storm King fight dragged on, the utility had high hopes that the conservationists and the public at large would support plans for "clean" nuclear power. These hopes were quickly dashed.

First, Con Ed made the awful mistake of launching a trial balloon in order to gauge public opinion on the location of nuclear plants in populated centers. Con Ed applied to the Atomic Energy Commission for a license to build a one million kilowatt nuclear plant at Ravenswood, in New York City's Queen's Borough. Citizens, the state, city officials and media commenced a storm of protest, basing their opposition essentially on inchoate fears about the dangers of radiation. The Committee Against Nuclear Power Plants in New York City was organized. The scenic preservationists rallied to the side of those alarmed by the various specters that continue to haunt nuclear power. Even the first AEC chairman, David E. Lilienthal, got into the act, saying that he would not think of living next door to a nuclear plant. Con Ed withdrew its application in early 1964, after doing more than its share to get the nuclear debate going on a rational rather than emotional level.

After its Ravenswood balloon collapsed and while it was still embroiled in the Cornwall dispute and under growing pressure to clean up its filthy air emissions, Con Ed looked completely to nuclear power to solve the problem of future power needs. Its first nuclear plant at Indian Point had not been an unqualified success. A prototype, the 260,000-kilowatt plant developed all kinds of bugs. There were endless design and construction changes resulting in delays. Costs rose from $57 million to a final total of $136 million. Even so, Indian Point was considered a worthwhile venture, the forerunner of a string of such plants that would produce seventy-five percent of Con Ed's power by 1980. A second and much larger nuclear plant at Indian Point (873,000 kilowatts) was counted on for delivery of peak load power as early as May, 1969.

Meanwhile, Con Ed was continually embarrassed over its enormous share of New York's air pollution. The company's coal and oil burning plants were producing about half of the sulfur oxides and nearly a fifth of the particulates that were hanging over the city, and on Thanksgiving Day, 1966, these were blamed for 50 deaths. By 1967, Con Ed had spent $100 million to control emissions from the fossil fuel plants, mainly by installing electrostatic precipitators to check fly ash and taller stacks to disperse sulfur oxides.

The company's clean air campaign was accelerated dramatically by Charles Luce. He is justifiably proud that Con Ed was three years ahead of the city's deadline which required that the sulfur content of fuel must be one percent or lower. He has accurately noted that the city is far behind Con Ed, for example, in controlling emissions from its own incinerators.

Con Ed was not able to pay for clean air controls without passing along the costs. During the past decade, rate hikes have cost New York consumers over $100 million and have generally aroused further opposition to Con Ed. The only way to reduce these costs, Luce held, was to convert quickly to nuclear power which consumes fuel much more cheaply and which is not fraught with constant fuel shortages and fluctuating fuel prices.

So in the spring of 1968, Luce considered at least four possible sites for nuclear plants and hoped to be able to have an operating nuclear plant on one of them by 1974. As it turned out, each site has drawbacks and it is unlikely that any one of the four will have a plant on it by 1978. It takes about six years to build a plant. In addition, construction costs and technical difficulties have continued to be a persistent handicap.

The first site, on Davids Island, just off New Rochelle on Long Island Sound, is so close to the metropolis that even AEC officials had misgivings. The second site was in Montrose, three miles below Indian Point. It was immediately opposed by the Kolping Society, a lay Catholic group which owned the center of the property. The Hudson River Fisherman's Association also would not accept still another nuclear plant in the Indian Point vicinity. When and if three Indian Point plants are in operation, as now planned, over two million gallons of hot water per minute will be poured into the river.

The third possibility was Trap Rock, a quarry excavation at Verplanck, between Montrose and Indian Point. However, the price of the land was considered "staggering." Finally, Con Ed looked to Bowline Point, not far downstream from Montrose on the west bank of the Hudson. This was not an ideal site because its bedrock is not close to the surface, and transmission lines would be needed to cross the river.

As he tried to cope with the power crisis during the summer of 1969, Charles Luce could barely conceal his frustration. He had come to Con Ed an enlightened public official who believed in opening the channels of communication to the public and, above all, in precise long-term planning. But he had been blocked on all fronts. Even Indian Point Two had missed the deadline when its state operating permit was delayed by litigation and the plant contractor was bogged down in a labor dispute. The utility also had a construction permit for an Indian Point Three but this proposal, too, faced a citizen's suit. Con Ed had resorted to gas turbine generators for emergencies. These were small, noisy, expensive to run, unreliable and required constant maintenance. In addition to these difficulties, in July 1971, the Federal Court of Appeals ruled that Indian Point Two must be subject to new environmental studies under the National Environmental Protection Act. Con Ed's Luce contended that every month this plant was delayed, it cost electricity users between two and three million dollars.

On July 22, 1969, Luce wrote a letter (see Appendix A) to New York Mayor John Lindsay recounting Con Ed's then recent difficulties, the company's record in attaining cleaner air and explaining the reasons for turning to a last resort, one that Con Ed had previously told the public would be avoided at all cost. This plan was to increase the fossil fuel facilities of the Astoria site by 1,600 megawatts. It was certain to incur the wrath of the Citizens for Clean Air, Inc., and would undoubtedly arouse opposition in the city government. That Luce should have to take such pains to state his case reveals the extent to which a giant utility becomes enmeshed in the

CON ED: AN ECOLOGICAL PERSPECTIVE / 51

political structure of a large metropolitan region. It also illustrates the role that electric energy plays in the social and economic well-being of the community.

In substance, Luce pointed out in the letter that Con Ed had been more than responsible in honoring its pledge to reduce its dirty air emissions, a promise which it had made to the city in a 1966 memorandum. The utility had gone to a low sulfur oil—from two percent to one percent and, when such fuel was obtainable, to .37 percent. The company was also converting coal-fired generators to oil wherever feasible. Even by adding to its fossil-fuel facilities at Astoria, burning low-sulfur fuel oil and cleaning up the existing coal furnaces, Con Ed would attain its goal of reducing fly ash emissions by sixty-four percent and sulfur oxides by seventy-one percent in a period of ten years from that time, that is, 1976. In order to cope with increasing emergencies and because of so many "slippages" in construction schedules, Con Ed had spent $80 million on gas and light oil-fired turbines that would put out 750 megawatts, Luce told the Mayor. However, he emphasized, that additions to Astoria would be necessary by 1974.

The letter ended with a strong pitch for nuclear energy as the method of generation that "holds the greatest promise of enabling Con Edison to supply the immense new quantities of electric energy required by New York City and Westchester County with the least impact on the quality of the environment." If this carefully understated description of Con Ed's plans for new fossil fuel facilities in the already-dirty city was not enough to stir up the wrath of government and citizens, Con Ed delivered another blow in August. It applied to the Public Service Commission for an increase of 14.0 percent on residential electricity rates and 16.9 percent for commercial customers. As the summer ended, 1.9 million new shares of the utility's common stock were offered. During this period, Con Ed's stock dropped to an eleven-year low. With that kind of ironic perfection New Yorkers are accustomed to, a feeder cable at the East 14th Street substation went out which, in turn, stopped the stock ticker of the New York Stock Exchange.

In September, 1920, the PSC granted Con Ed *some* increase

in rates—4.0 percent for residential users and 15.5 percent for commercial users, about $90 million of $119 million which was requested. But by this time, Con Ed's agonies had only grown more intense. Luce had gone before the city administration to plead this case for Astoria and air quality. He ended up with a compromise solution of 800 megawatts, half of what Con Ed originally wanted. Clean Air advocates complained vociferously that the city's Environmental Protection Agency had caved in. A Committee To Stop Con Ed's Pollution Project was born. It had been a dreadful summer. Indian Point One went out with a defect in the cooling system. Big Allis halted again, causing Con Ed's capability to drop some thirteen percent, just in time for the August heat. Power was imported from Canada and the Tennessee Valley Authority, but there was still a considerable amount of disruption. Voltage reductions were ordered at least fifteen times. In three cases, these reductions went to eight percent, a situation under which some kinds of electric service motors may be strained, old wiring insulation burned, and x-ray clarity reduced. Once, sixty-five blocks were blacked out. Subway runs were cut down. People were implored to use their air conditioners sparingly and, if possible, not at all. Con Ed, once called by *Fortune* Magazine "the company you love to hate," could not escape its role as prime target of common discontent.

It did not help one bit when in mid-summer, 1970, an atmosphere inversion created an ever-thickening blanket of pollutants over New York City. John Noble Wilford, a *New York Times* science writer, submitted a strong column of news analysis on the price of technology. "When the blanket of hot air settled over the city, trapping pollution below," he wrote, "the city's residents turned on air-conditioning units and, not wanting to get out in the heat, probably watched more television. Then, according to some city officials, when subway service was curtailed to conserve power, more people decided to drive to work, thus adding more fumes to the pollution."

The scenarios played out in 1971 were, in truth and without exaggeration, frightening. The one most precisely thought out was provided by William K. Jones, one of the five members of the PSC. He prepared a seventy-seven page report which explored all contingencies in the event of a severe power shortage and made recommendations for reducing or even cutting power entirely in certain areas. This document spells out how, during a crisis, electricity is to be kept running for communications, transportation system, hospitals, water service, sewage disposal, police and fire department operations, high rise buildings where elevators are the key links, and the bridges that connect New York City to the outside world. The term, for Jones, is "load shedding," a state of emergency that Henry Adams could never have forseen when he gazed with admiration upon the dynamo.

First Jones noted that peak demand on Con Ed's system during the 1971 summer was expected to be 8,150 megawatts while Con Ed was capable of generating 8,802 megawatts. Adding 1,020 megawatts from outside power contracts, including four new barge mounted gas turbines that could deliver 636 megawatts, this brought the capacity up to 9,822 megawatts. (At midsummer, not all the gas turbines had yet gone on the line and Jones' figure for imports was 100 megawatts too high, according to Con Ed.)

These figures must then be put into the equation that is called "lost capacity." This is computed by determining how much a generator has lost from its "nameplate" rating as it got older, the average amount of power outages, probable failures because of deferred repairs, and possible losses due to major breakdowns like the maladies suffered over recent summers by "Big Allis." According to one report, cited by Jones, Con Ed would have to subtract 2,0075 megawatts in "lost capacity" if the Ravenswood No. 3 generator (Big Allis) were in service and 3,075 megawatts if it were not. Either way, Jones saw that Con Ed would have a power deficit since its capacity would be either 7,527 megawatts or 6,527 megawatts, depending on Big Allis' performance. Obviously, Con Ed would have to resort to various kinds of savings and reductions during the difficult days of summer.

If indeed there is a crisis like the ones described at the beginning of this chapter, Con Ed does have a battle plan. The company procedures can be generally summarized in this order, as the crisis gets worse. Generators are brought to "sustained rating," that is, almost full tilt. Outside power is purchased. Gas turbines are turned on. Newer stations go to short-time ratings, i.e. maximum output for short periods. Leased boiler plants start sending steam into office air conditioning systems so that Con Ed can use the steam in electric generators. Con Ed cuts the power in its own substantial office and plant complex. Voltage is reduced by three percent which amounts to 185 megawatts. Telephone and mass media appeals go out first to large customers then to everybody. Voltage is reduced five percent or another 125 megawatts. Con Ed asks the state for help, which may mean releasing water from Lake Ontario. Voltage is reduced eight percent or by another 185 megawatts, making a total of 495. Older stations go to maximum ratings. Power is shut off in certain less densely settled residential sections. Subway service is reduced.

There are elaborate implementations of this battle order, applying parts or all of it, depending on how the day is going.

One of the most hair-raising of the scenarios worked out by Jones has "Big Allis" out of service, in addition to generally adverse conditions in Con Ed's equipment and on the weather front. Jones gets a deficit of 2,546 megawatts. All of the steps just described, including an eight percent voltage reduction, are taken, but there remains a 1,557 megawatt gap. All that can be done then is to shut off power to places like Brooklyn, the Bronx, Queens, Staten Island and Westchester. Jones thought that such adversities were unlikely. However, he wrote, "It is not unreasonable, in light of Consolidated Edison's unfortunate history, to keep one eye in on the most disadvantageous possibilities." The possibilities continued to become realities during the summer of 1971: Big Allis went out of service on the same day that all four of the gas turbine emergency generators failed along with minor failures in three other units.

What can Con Ed do? What are the lessons to be learned from this awful predicament, this tightening web of troubles that besets the mightiest electric company? What does it mean for all of us?

In a speech to college students, who often invite Luce into their midst and with whom he enjoys talking, Con Ed's president gave this answer, "Solutions to all of these environmental problems and others that might be mentioned, must be found in one or both of two ways: 1) Improve the technology of producing and transmitting electricity so that they cause less damage to the environment, or 2) Reduce the use of electricity, either by rationing or voluntarily."

Having trouble with the first, Con Ed has moved aggressively down the second road. On May 3, 1971, the company did an unheard-of thing. At a City Hall news conference with Mayor Lindsay, Luce announced that Con Ed would give up advertising the benefits of electricity, would stop extolling electrical appliances and other gadgets as the highest joys of living. The utility would also conduct a "save a watt' campaign and thereby, perhaps, lessen Big Allis' suffering. Mayor Lindsay congratulated Con Ed's move: "It recognizes not only the need for short term rational reductions of power consumption, but also helps place in sharper relief complex questions about the need for power and its uses, and its impact on the environment."

How do you save a watt? Con Ed urged people to do the following:

1. Turn off air conditioners during the day when no one is home.

2. When using air conditioners, select a moderate or medium setting rather than a high one.

3. Keep windows closed and blinds and shades adjusted to keep out the sun during the day, so that air conditioners do not have to work too hard when they are in use.

4. Keep lights off during daylight hours, except for safety, health and comfort reasons.

5. Plan to run major and small appliances before 8 a.m. and after 6 p.m.

6. *Use dishwashers just once a day, after the evening meal.*

7. *Plan washer and dryer loads for evenings and weekends, if possible. Do one full load instead of many small loads.*

8. *Never leave an electric range or oven on when not actually in use.*

9. *Turn off television and radio sets when you are not looking or listening.*

10. *If possible save occasional jobs like vacuum cleaning or working with power tools until the weekend.*

11. *When buying an air conditioner, look for the right size unit for your needs. Select a unit that gives you the maximum number of BTU's for every watt used.*

Did it work? It seemed to. By July of 1971, Con Ed detected a savings of 300 to 350 megawatts from the year before, not counting an estimated 150 megawatt reduction attributed to an economic slump. Luce told his experts to figure out other ways of saving electricity, such as getting offices to minimize their use of fluorescent lights which cause heat thereby counteracting the effect of air conditioning and, consequently, squandering electricity in two ways. His own office, it was noted, was lit only by the sunlight. He explained how, if you use a number of separate switches on lighting banks, you could select just those lights you needed without having to turn them all on just to light your desk area.

It would seem that at last, we are getting to the roots of the problem: we are getting people to curb their appetites for electricity. But is this enough? How much time will it buy? Isn't it necessary in order to solve the long term crisis for us to get back to Luce's first point, finding a technological breakthrough which will make big changes in the *system*?

S. David Freeman, cited previously in this book, has advocated a change in electric rates that, instead of giving incentives to burn more power, would penalize large users. "The economy is apt to generate demands for energy that will be difficult to meet even without rate structures that add to the problem by encouraging faster growth," Freeman said in a late 1970 speech. "With fuel costs rising by leaps and bounds, new plants costing more than existing facilities, gains in efficiency at a halt and even slipping, the cost of new money double the embedded cost of capital, and new plants requiring expensive environmental protection, I believe it is fair to suggest that the faster we grow the faster rates will go up."

Con Ed's Luce has been edging towards Freeman's position, as reflected in new rate applications presented to the Public Service Commission in the spring of 1971. Those who are called "end block" customers, because their large volume of power use falls in the last or end rate category, would be asked to pay higher rates for increased consumption of power.

But this approach also poses a dilemma. Con Ed's "end block" customers sued the utility in July, 1971, for imposing an unfair burden by reversing the tradition of cheaper rates for large users. As put by Luce in an interview, "Sure, the economy of scale no longer applies to Con Ed and the city of New York. Volume demands for power are now terribly painful to meet and the costs difficult to bear. But our largest customer is the transit authority. Our second largest is the city with schools and streets to light up. These customers are the public. Is it fair to penalize them?" On the other hand, Luce wanted to make clear, "If we really mean what we say about the costs [of environmental quality] being born by the users, then the costs of electric power are going to have to go up."

It is difficult to make a fair judgement of Con Ed and Luce's performance and all too simple to blame the utility for the mess it is in. The company's financial plight is not within the scope of this discussion, but it is obvious that Con Ed is plagued by conditions that militate against cost efficiencies. Some of these factors were cited in a report by the FPC in December, 1969: "The highly developed Consolidated Edison area tends to limit load growth, to favor commercial over industrial development, to impose serious constraints on development of new power facilities, and to create extraordinary financial burdens for the utility. The island and peninsular configuration of the service area poses major problems of access to neighboring facilities.

These factors impose on the utility a need for extraordinarily careful and thorough planning, and suggest that lead times for getting facilities into service can be expected to be longer here than on most other major utility systems."

Con Ed's 66,000 miles of underground transmission lines—the longest utility system in the world—are inordinately expensive to maintain, twice as costly as the maintenance of generating facilities. Con Ed is New York's largest payer of property taxes (in 1970, over 200 million dollars.) Its capital expenditures total more than $250 million a year, so its interest costs in obtaining capital financing are enormous, often exceeding returns on capital. The public outcry against Con Ed which goes back even before the memorable battles over rates with Mayor Fiorello La Guardia, along with other political controversies involving the utility, have not helped to make Con Ed an inviting investment.

To be sure, Con Ed officials have consistently underestimated resistence—by the public and conservationists, as well as the city and state—to their various plans to provide power. Not enough alternatives have been drafted by Con Ed strategists. But have these alternatives been available? Does a forum exist where they could have been reasonably discussed? There is no clear answer to the former question. To the latter one the answer is no.

On August 13, 1969, just after he wrote his letter to Mayor Lindsay, Luce appealed to Governor Nelson Rockefeller. He also presented the governor with Con Ed's ten year plan to meet growing power demands. He asked that the state get together with New York City, the Public Service Commission, the FPC and Westchester County to conduct a "coordinated review" of Con Ed's predicament and future. Since then Luce has called for a single state agency to review and make decisions upon all utility plans for the types and locations of power plants. At present, he has noted, "the utility must go to a multitude, perhaps 15 or 20 local and state agencies plus several federal agencies. Any one of these agencies can say no, but in saying no cannot at the same time say yes to an alternative site. Perhaps this hit-or-miss, catch-as-catch-can method of plant siting was adequate to the energy and environmental needs of yesterday. Today it is a costly and dangerous anachronism."

George C. Lodge, an associate professor at the Harvard Graduate School of Business Administration, has written that Con Ed's problems "derive from the political structures that surround it and the tension, confusion, and competition of interests they embody." Con Ed is inextricably caught in a web between the city which determines company costs and services and the state which approves rate structures. For this reason, Lodge sees Con Ed as simply not "properly constituted, in political terms," to work its way out of the impasse. "Would it not make more sense," he wrote, "for the New York State Power Authority or a new northeast regional public power authority to be charged with the task of power production, leaving to private companies the distribution of power on a decentralized basis to meet local consumer needs."

Luce does not buy Lodge's argument, at least for the moment. When interviewed in the summer of 1971, he felt that such a solution would only shift the problems and the blame to a structure which is institutionally and bureaucratically even more unsuited to cope with the dilemma of power. He thought his proposal for a unified regulatory system ought to be given a try first. (As will be noted in Chapter 4, the authors do not entirely agree.)

Meantime, where are those technological breakthroughs? Luce does not see them, at least not for several decades. For the foreseeable future, he has put his faith and backing in nuclear power, although he has misgivings about thermal problems—both in the water and air. "I think we must realize that even if successful in developing dry towers (for cooling), we are really only providing a short term solution to a long-term problem by changing the heat rejection reservoir from water to air," he has said. "The real solution is to increase plant efficiency. While the atmosphere may be the ultimate heat sink, it is not an infinite heat sink."

The disposal of nuclear wastes does not dissuade Luce. He accepts the AEC's answer that nuclear wastes can be solidified and put in abandoned salt mines or in underground salt formations. The AEC has said that by the year 2000, the projected waste load would require no more than 1,200 to 3,000 acres of salt mines or roughly 770,000 cubic feet—a space equivalent 100x100x100 feet. And, the AEC has maintained, there are 400,000 acres of U.S. land underlaid by salt formations.

Luce sees the so-called "fast-breeder" type of nuclear unit as being the answer to the thermal problem. It should have a superior thermal efficiency and be able to generate as much fuel in ten years as it used over the same period (see page 76). The trouble is that federally sponsored research and development does not anticipate a fast breeder pilot plant before 1980, making operating plants unlikely before 1990.

Looking at Con Ed as a microcosm of the national dilemma of power does not lead anyone to a promised land of easy answers. Instead, Con Ed's difficulties as well as Luce's mood of deep concern ought to flash a clear warning signal.

The technological innovations we have always counted upon to bail us out are not, in this case, immediately forthcoming. Our best men are whipsawed and nearing exhaustion; our political, economic and scientific institutions have proven unequal to the task. The energy crisis casts a darkening shadow on all of us and on the future of all our institutions.

CHAPTER 4

TO KEEP
THE LIGHTS
BURNING

In any discussion about the energy crisis, it is tempting to take a simple stand. One might say, for example, that there ought to be a law that sets enforceable limits on the consumption of electricity by homeowners, offices and factories alike. Effective as such a statute might be, however, it would not be possible politically or technically to impose. Certainly it is likely and even desirable that someday the large users of power will have to pay an energy tax, a surcharge that is levied against a progressively higher volume of use. But one must first stop to consider the total energy picture before insisting that electricity be limited across the board.

When and if electric-powered rapid transit systems become the main means of transport, first in cities and then throughout the country, *more electricity will be needed while, at the same time, total fuel combustion will be much less.* When U.S. industries are finally forced to recycle wastes in order to save valuable natural resources, electric energy will be needed in the reclaiming processes—crushing, grinding, separating, melting, reconstituting and so forth. The point is that in the entire energy equation, after all the pros and cons of environmental quality have been considered, such as obtaining cleaner air and water, using land more efficiently and conserving resources, electricity plays a major role. We are still left with no simple answers.

Even so, there is plenty of room for improvement. Institutions and policies can and must be changed to cope with the problems of power. More and more environmental controls must be applied to plants and transmission line locations. Laws and incentives must be devised that will bring about significant savings in power consumption. Existing methods of generation must be made much more clean and efficient. Finally, "breakthroughs" must be sought *and, at the same time, no long-term commitments should be made to any one or more methods of producing power that presently appear promising.* In the judgment of the authors, this is an imperative. At some time in the future, it is hoped—indeed, assumed—that our energy policymakers will be able to chart a course with some degree of confidence and certainty. But now, the bets that are being placed on one alternative or another—coal gasification, nuclear power, natural gas and so forth—are all terribly risky. There has been such a paucity of research and development by both private industry and government that caution is the order of the day. Already, the price paid for "progress" has been far too high.

Policy Recommendations

At Congressional hearings in June, 1969, Lee White, then head of the Federal Power Commission, testified that "existing procedures for reconciling the need for new facilities and environmental protection are inadequate. There is not enough disclosure by the utilities of what they plan to do. There is not enough consultation among all those interested utilities and between the utilities and the various land use and environmental planning agencies. There is no clear-cut procedure by which, once all the consultations have been undertaken, final decisions can be made which permit construction and avoid stalemate." Mr. White was talking, of course, about the rising tide of opposition to power plants based on environmental considerations. Since then, the statutory situation has not changed much, although the climate has improved significantly. A few states have taken progressive steps which will be described later in this chapter. And there are various proposals before Congress that would unify and coordinate the planning of the nation's power needs.

On May 3, 1971 the U.S. Senate passed a resolution that set up a National Energy Policy Subcommittee, under the Committee on Interior and Insular Affairs. Composed of members of every senate committee involved in energy affairs, this body is mandated to report to the nation by the end of 1972 with a preliminary analysis of the energy crisis and what can be done about it. On June 4, 1971, President Nixon delivered an administration message that outlined energy problems as well as some proposals. Separate parts of the message will be taken up as they become pertinent later in this chapter. As a matter of policy, the president proposed a single energy authority at the federal level which would be an arm of the Department of Natural Resources, which is itself the hoped-for result of a proposed cabinet reorganization. Thus the energy planning activities of the FPC, the Atomic Energy Commission, various Interior bureaus, the Tennessee Valley Authority, the Rural Electrification Administration, etc., would all be combined under one roof. According to the presidential message, "The establishment of this new entity would provide a focal point where energy policy in the executive branch could be harmonized and rationalized." Just how this super-body would exert actual control over the fragmented plans of some 3,600 utilities was not spelled out. And, of course, it could not be realized until the Interior Department finally became a Department of Natural Resources. Until that time, the president said, he would rely on his energy policy staff for an overview on energy questions.

The Nixon message also skirted some very delicate areas—notably the key questions of fuel policy, such as what to do with the oil import quota system—which are at the very root of energy considerations. Neither did the message note the interaction of energy and transportation policies that results from fuel commonalities. As John Lear, the *Saturday Review*'s science editor, justly noted, "In terms of horsepower per pound, experts say the energy in the oil would be more efficiently used if the freight were carried in railroad trains drawn by oil-burning locomotives. Does the government wish to encourage rail traffic over truck traffic? The president gave no sign."

One way or another, the federal government will have to act in the public interest and acquire the final authority over plans to meet the requirements of electric power throughout the nation. Some experts have advocated that the government take a radical course. John T. Miller, a Georgetown University law professor, proposed in the May, 1970, issue of the *Fordham Law Review* that federally constituted authorities take over all of the nation's generating and transmitting facilities, leaving the utilities the business of distributing and marketing power. Such an arrangement, it is argued, would not only coordinate energy planning, but would relieve the utilities from the economic and environmental pressures so vividly apparent in the case of Con Ed. Harvard business professor George C. Lodge, whose case studies were referred to earlier, has worked out this scenario: 1) Congress charters investor-owned *regional* public utility corporations to generate and transmit power on an interstate basis. 2) The existing facilities are incorporated within the regional corporations by being exchanged at book value for securities in the regional firm. 3) A federal agency is given licensing and rate-setting authority over the regional power producer. 4) The existing utilities become wholesale customers of the regional corporations.

This whole idea gained standing when it was advanced at a senate hearing by S. David Freeman, then the president's energy policy staff director. Abundant evidence showed "that there are large savings to be achieved in really integrating planning, construction, and operation of generation and transmission facilities over a broad region of the nation," Freeman said, while large companies have no inherent advantages over smaller ones when it comes to marketing electricity. "A small distributor can achieve unit costs that are as low as a large distributor," he said. Freeman went on to suggest that a national power grid be established to supplant the power pools and other arrangements that utilities make to serve their regions more efficiently. Regional generating and transmitting companies would be fitted to the grid, selling power to small distributors who would remain close and responsive to their customers and who would become more profitable operations when finally rid of rising capital costs. The regional companies would gain a measure of security by being backed by the federal government. According to Freeman, the arrangement would provide fairer competition under the free enterprise system: "Power distributors would not be in the generating business and could compete on equal terms and with assurance of bulk power supply from strong neutral sources. The regional transmission grid could be made available to any potential supplier—it would be an electrical toll highway, so to speak—and generating companies could compete for the distributors' growth."

Environmental Controls

A great deal is known about the environmental controls deemed necessary for the present generation of power plants and facilities planned in the near future. The trouble is that a citizen has to know where to look. Restrictions pertaining to power plant siting appear under the Federal Air and Water Quality Acts, the Atomic Energy Act of 1954, the Fish and Wildlife Coordination Act, the National Historic Preservation Act of 1966, the Federal Power Act and in numerous state laws. As this book was being written, the Nixon administration proposed a power plant siting law to establish federal environmental guidelines that would be carried out by single state agencies. The proposed bill would also force utilities to prepare long-term plans and to disclose publically, at least five years in advance, plans for both plants and transmission lines so that open hearings could be held in good time.

The state energy authority described in the Nixon proposal

would consolidate all the different stages of review at the local and state level. The Department of Natural Resources would lay down the law for the federal government if a state failed to establish an agency and procedures under the bill.

This proposal, which has some variations, was the result of two thorough reports by the Energy Policy Staff of the Office of Science and Technology. Each one is well worth reading. The first, *Considerations Affecting Steam Power Plant Site Selection,* published at the end of 1968, was a comprehensive analysis of environmental tradeoffs, with chapters on nuclear plants, air and water pollution, aesthetic considerations, land-use and transmission line problems. The second report, *Electric Power and the Environment,* publiched in August, 1970, brought the earlier study up to date and went heavily into institutional arrangements. The "Environmental Protection Checklist and Guidelines for Site Selection" from that report can be found in Appendix B of this book. In brief, what environmental standards already exist under which the public can seek relief from the existence of plants, or the construction of new plants, which degrade the environment?

Air emissions from power plants are subject to state air quality regulations implemented under the Federal Air Quality Act. However, many new plants—particularly those burning fossil fuel—are planned outside the present network of air quality districts which are primarily airsheds in urban regions. The Southwest coal-fired plants described in Chapter II are an example. Moreover, power plants are not subject to review under the air quality statute until *after* they are built—at a time when pressures mount up to grant exceptions and variances. Eventually, these loopholes will almost certainly be plugged by air quality legislation requiring national emission standards.

Under the 1970 Water Quality Act, a power plant cannot be licensed for construction until it is assured that the plant will comply with water quality guidelines, *including criteria for thermal discharges*. In other words, the AEC cannot license or give the go-ahead to a nuclear plant until the state water quality agency is satisfied that the proposal contains safeguards against thermal pollution. Radiological effects are still considered under the Atomic Energy Act of 1954.

Until tough federal legislation is passed that, in turn, will result in forceful state action to deal with power plant siting, the National Environmental Protection Act of 1970 remains the best tool (see page 39). Under this law, environmental impact statements are required from any federal agency involved in a project that could have an effect on the environment. The measure would apply to projects requiring FPC or AEC certification, to a plan dependent on fuel provided under a mining lease issued by a federal agency (e.g. the case in the Southwest controversy) and to a proposal that involves a construction or dredging permit issued by the Army Corps of Engineers. While the environmental impact statement is not in any way binding, it brings issues out into the open and can trigger public hearings. The Interior Department's delay in granting a pipeline permit to bring oil down from Alaska's North Slope was the result of a critical statement from the Geological Survey that, in turn, prompted an outcry from conservation-minded congressmen and senators.

As of mid-1970, at least six states—Maine, Washington, California, Maryland, New York and Vermont—had created new authorities to deal with power plant siting and transmission line routes. In Maine, an Environmental Improvement Commission has broad powers to rule on any large power development that might have a significant impact on the environment. Washington has created a Thermal Power Plant Site Evaluation Council. California has a similar arrangement. Maryland suspended all site acquisition and development for steam plants that had not begun by July 1, 1970, until a new board could conduct environmental impact studies and establish siting guidelines. New York's Public Service Commission has authority over transmission rights-of-way and a temporary state commission was assigned to recommend power plant siting laws to the 1971 legislature. In Vermont, the State Public Service Board has the power to deny certification to any proposed power plant that would not comply with air and water quality standards, would not fit in with the planned growth of a region and would not conform, in general, to aesthetic criteria brought up at public hearings.

Fuel Policies

Earlier in this book environmental considerations regarding various fuels were outlined. It was noted that certain fuels were cleaner than others and that market and policy influences often restricted the uses of these fuels. Low-sulfur, high-grade coal, for example, is in high demand in Europe and Japan for making steel. The U.S. oil industry receives government incentive and protection to the extent that, among other things, it is more profitable to refine crude oil into gasoline and light distillate products than into home heating oil or low-sulfur fuel for power plants. Some experts feel that the pressures of air quality legislation will produce a healthy market for low-sulfur oil and coal. That may or may not be the case. It hasn't happened yet. As an additional means of assuring supplies of clean fuel, in the authors' judgment, it would seem worthwhile to make production of a certain amount of such oil and coal a condition of any license or contract involving the federal government. The environmental pros and cons of an Alaskan pipeline are not going to be discussed again. But if such a pipeline is ultimately granted to bring all that oil down from Prudhoe Bay in the Arctic, the Interior Department ought to demand that, along with environmental safeguards, a certain percentage of the oil be refined into clean fuel for power generation. The same condition could apply to strip-mined coal taken from federal lands and to oil taken from beneath the continental shelf where state and/or federal approval is required.

It should be noted here that in order to cope with the short-term energy crisis—not to mention the long-term—President Nixon asked the Interior Department to open up more of the federal lands which are estimated to hold more than half the nation's remaining oil and gas reserves, about forty percent of our coal and uranium, eighty percent of our oil shale and sixty percent of our geothermal (e.g. underground steam) sources.

The administration also asked The Interior Department to step up leasing for oil and gas on the outer continental shelf. Even though environmental controls on offshore operations have been strengthened, there surely will be more accidents on the scale of the Santa Barbara and Gulf of Mexico disasters of 1969 and 1970.

It would appear far more foresighted for the federal government to amend or scrap entirely the oil quota system which has had the unanticipated effect of encouraging U.S. producers to squander rather than hold in reserve their resource stocks. Such a move would also allow much needed time to consider the long-term environmental impact of offshore drilling.

Energy Conservation

Nobody knows how much relief can be obtained if we all made a conscious effort to use less electricity; if rates were, in effect, reversed and a progressive energy tax applied to large users as penalties for excessive consumption; and if effluent charges were levied on manufacturing industries so that they are forced to produce products requiring less energy and, thereby, producing less of a waste problem (e.g. tin vs. aluminum cans). S. David Freeman has noted that the rate of growth in electricity consumption could be cut in half with austerity measures like these. He has urged a "war on waste in the use of energy and the beginning of an era of conservation in its use."

Previously, Con Ed's electricity conservation list was presented, telling citizens what they individually could do to save electricity. The American Institute of Architects has prepared a report showing how building design and construction changes could bring about significant savings. The report suggested that buildings be designed to take advantage of natural light and natural ventilation; that buildings be heated from systems serving many homes in common and using waste heat such as that from a municipal incinerator; that schools, industries and business offices look into the wastefulness of their lighting systems; that electrical luxury gadgets be discouraged; and that energy not be used in such nonessential ways as outdoor advertising in the form of neon signs, for example. Badly insulated buildings can allow a heat loss up to thirty percent. As this was written, the Federal Housing Administration was drafting new insulation standards for all federally insured homes. In New York, Mayor Lindsay's Interdepartmental Committee on Public Utilities has urged the city to require efficiency ratings for air conditioners. In a report, this group held that efficient air conditioners, as opposed to brands that are far less effective, could save the city up to 50,000 kilowatts during the peak hours of a hot summer day. It was expected that 250,000 new air conditioners would be installed for the summer of 1971 and would consume about 280,000 kilowatts of electricity. No analysis has been made of the savings that would result from maximum temperature settings on building heating thermostats or minimum settings on air conditioners. We may come to this. Certainly many buildings are far too warm in winter and far too cold in summer.

We have previously noted that Con Ed was gradually coming to the point of charging higher rates for a heavier volume of electric use. As S. David Freeman puts it, "What better way is there to give people an incentive to conserve energy than to make them pay more for wasting it." Certainly this would be fair to the average city resident who uses less than 300 kilowatt hours a month and is *not* the person causing power shortages.

For a time it was fashionable to blame electric toothbrushes for the power crisis. To be sure, the American household consumes a great deal more electricity than that of other nations, and considerably more than it used to. As we have seen, household use is by no means the major consumption factor, yet extragavance is extravagance whenever it is found: the culprits in your house are the elctric range, the dryer, and window air conditioners. Here is a list, compiled by the New York *Times,* of power in watts for common household appliances.

Electric Range 12,205
Laundry Dryer 4,855
Air Conditioner
  (window) 1,565
Dishwasher 1,200
Fry Pan 1,195
Toaster 1,145
Iron 1,090
Coffee Maker 895
Blender 385
Hair Dryer 380
Refrigerator-
  Freezer 325
Laundry Washer 285-510
Television Set 235
Fan (window) 225
Ventilator 150-200
Mixer 125
Can Opener 90
Sewing Machine 75
Tuner-Amplifier 50
Toothbrush 7

At present, most utilities reduce the unit price of power as a customer's volume of use increases. As Charles Luce has pointed out, the so-called economy of scale in which the more power you make the more cheap and profitable it is to make it is no longer applicable to most power companies. Their existing facilities are strained. Capital costs to add to these facilities, often just to be able to take care of peak hour demands and to include the price of environmental safeguards, are extremely high. And yet, as the Nixon administration energy message noted, "One reason we use energy so lavishly today is that the price of energy does not include all of the social costs of producing it. The costs incurred in protecting the environment and the health and safety of workers, for example, are part of the real cost of producing energy—but they are not now all included in the price of the product. If they were added to that price, we could expect that some of the waste in the use of energy would be eliminated."

"Reversing" rates would be one way of paying the bill for environmental costs. Another of course would be the levying of an effluent charge based on the volume of sulfur oxide or soot emissions from power plants. If this were done, utilities would certainly pass some of it along in rate revisions.

Con Ed's Luce has also suggested a federal excise tax on all electricity use. The tax revenues would go to a trust fund, similar to the Highway Trust Fund which is supported by gasoline taxes. The trust fund would be allocated to research and development activities in the energy fields.

Energy Efficiency

The U.S. Naval Base at Norfolk, Virginia, draws both heat and electricity from the incinerator in which it burns 140 tons of refuse per day. According to a report in *Saturday Review,* the Navy saves $50,000 a year with its special furnace and generates 50,000 pounds of steam an hour. The incinerator residues are used for landfill.

The Union Electric Co. in mid-1971 announced that it was building a furnace and boiler unit that will burn the refuse of the city of St. Louis while generating 140 megawatts of power. The city is delighted to find such a solution to its waste disposal problems and the electric company, on the basis of careful engineering studies, thinks that the system will be economic.

In France, Parisians have for years produced heat and power out of garbage. In Sundbyberg, Sweden, a marvelous vacuum system sucks housewives' garbage bags into a sorting processor and finally a furnace where the combustion of refuse heats a 1,1000-unit apartment complex. The system is provided with effective controls against air pollution and bad odors. It has proven efficient and economical.

Whether such compact inventions are suited to American communities and American living habits is an unanswered question. But if the approach works for the 65,000 Navy men and their dependents at Norfolk it certainly should be encouraged and tried in our congested urban centers where the energy crisis is most severe. In Palo Alto, California, the Combustion Power Co. has been developing, under a federal grant, an electricity generating trash incinerator that is supposed to burn 400 tons a day, the output of 160,000 people, while producing 15,000 kilowatts of power. The BTU heating value of this furnace called the CPU 400 is about half that of high grade coal. Nevertheless, the sacrifice in heating efficiency is immaterial compared to the environmental economy of such a unit. Federal officials cannot wait until the CPU 400 is on the line and the company's assertions put to the test. Marvelous efficiency would result if these furnaces were linked to garbage conveyance systems like the Swedish vacuum tubes. The power would help in peak periods and might even fill a larger gap. Certainly there is no question but that great efficiencies can be achieved by recycling wastes—from garbage to industrial by-products, as well as through "clean" incineration. Iron, lead, aluminum and other metals reclaimed from waste often can be reconstituted in various forms with far less energy consumed than in production processes from raw materials. What is more, if the recycling process includes the generation of power from burning previously unreusable refuse, the savings are multiplied.

Incorporating the principles and technologies just described, so-called energy centers may in the future provide the solution to industrial energy needs. In such a complex (see diagram), an industrial hub, agricultural center and power plant might be interconnected so that the by-products and wastes of one fed the other. At this point, such ideas are visionary and untried. Moreover, environmental side effects might be unusually aggravating. We won't know until such an agro-industrial complex is built by itself or as part of a new town.

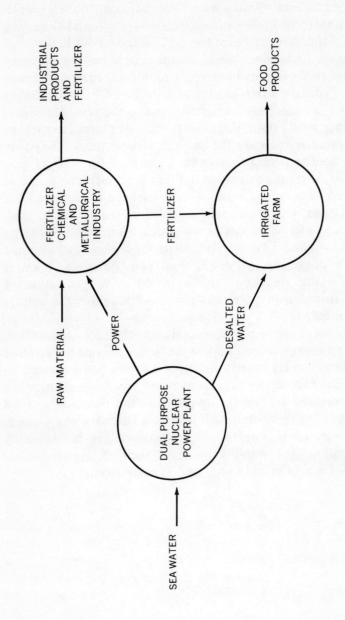

Agro-industrial energy complex

Improving Existing Technologies

Until there is that much-sought-for breakthrough in energy production, and while energy conservation and efficiency are being achieved to the utmost, there is a fair amount of room for improving the present methods. The dirtiest forms of power generation can be cleaned up considerably. The thermal efficiency of nuclear plants can be increased significantly. And methods of converting resources to fuel can be devised to produce cleaner burning fuel.

The best example of the latter approach is the government supported effort to find ways of converting coal to natural gas. In conjunction with the federal government, the American Gas Association and the Institute of Gas Technology have been supporting several projects for utilizing gas in large-scale energy production and in small-scale heating and air-conditioning systems. The most promising, thus far, has been the development of a pilot plant in Chicago that produces daily 1.5 million cubic feet of clean gas from seventy-five tons of coal. This so-called Hygas process is not expected to leave the pilot stage soon, however, and a big commercial operation to produce up to 250 million cubic feet of gas daily is unlikely until the end of this decade. Even so, with the supply of natural gas so critical and with coal reserves so great, gasification of coal— and perhaps, eventually, liquification—is most promising.

Even if fossil fuel power plants are made clean with sulfur oxide and soot controls, even if clean fuels can be made from our great reserves of coal and, to a lesser extent, from oil, the government is committed heavily to nuclear power. In the authors' judgment, safe nuclear power should be thoroughly explored for all its possibilities, but it would be unfortunate if the nation became so committed to nukes that it was practically and politically impossible to turn, in the next few decades, to another mode of power such as solar energy.

As indicated earlier in this book, there are as yet many disturbing unanswered questions concerning nuclear power. But President Nixon, following the lead of his advisers and the enthusiasm of the planners at the AEC, has committed the nation heavily to nuclear technology. The great hope for a decade from now is the so-called fast-breeder reactor which has a high thermal efficiency and which uses other fissionable materials, besides the increasingly scarce uranium 235, and which will produce more fuel than it consumes—or at least as much. Fast-breeder technology seems to be well understood, compared to thermonuclear technology (fusion), which is not even known to be possible. However, even with accelerated research support from the federal government, a commercial fast-breeder demonstration plant is not expected until 1980, which means that widespread construction and operation of such plants probably will not come for another decade after that. Moreover, the environmental hazards associated with fast-breeders may well be more troublesome than those plaguing today's nukes. There is no assurance at this point that troublesome quantities of radioactive wastes as well as thermal discharges, in spite of greater thermal efficiency, will not result with the advent of fast-breeder plants. Moreover, many scientists contend that this type of nuclear plant will have inherently greater potential for accidents resulting from exposure to radiation.

One method for improving the efficiency of conventional fossil fuel plants by utilizing extreme heat for more efficient use of the steam of cycle, is referred to as magnetohydrodynamics (MHD). According to the most recent testimony by government experts at congressional hearings, MHD is several decades away from realization. And even then, as shown in the diagram, it is expected to add no more than ten percent efficiency to the conventional cycle. Ultimately the method could even be employed to top off the steam cycle of the present type of light-water nuclear plant. MHD plants with a seventy-five percent thermal efficiency have been conceived as theoretical possibilities. Using this principle, hot, ionized gas would be passed through a magnetic field and electricity would be drawn from electrodes placed in that field. Used to top the steam cycle, MHD generators simply would take extremely high temperature gases directly without having to use a supplemental steam turbine.

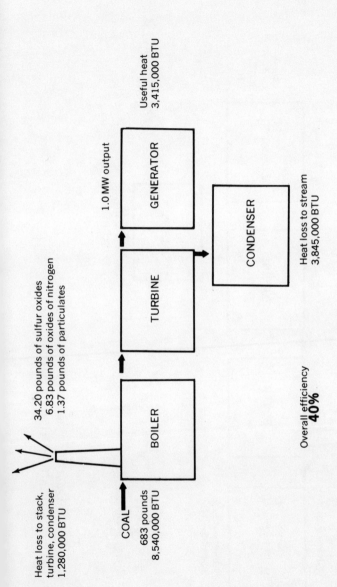

Heat loss to stack, turbine, condenser
1,280,000 BTU

34.20 pounds of sulfur oxides
6.83 pounds of oxides of nitrogen
1.37 pounds of particulates

COAL
683 pounds
8,540,000 BTU

BOILER

TURBINE

GENERATOR

CONDENSER

1.0 MW output

Useful heat
3,415,000 BTU

Heat loss to stream
3,845,000 BTU

Overall efficiency
40%

Conventional coal-burning scheme

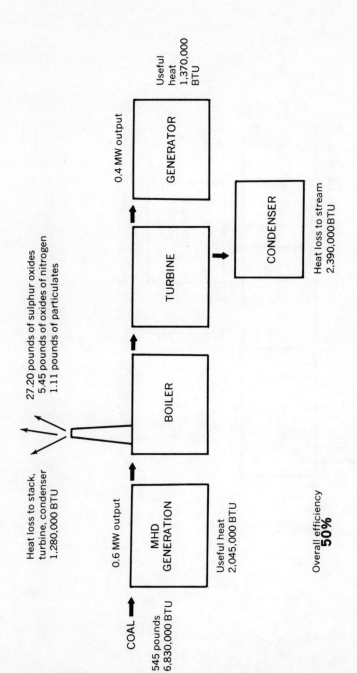

27.20 pounds of sulphur oxides
5.45 pounds of oxides of nitrogen
1.11 pounds of particulates

Useful heat 1,370,000 BTU

0.4 MW output

GENERATOR

CONDENSER

Heat loss to stream 2,390,000BTU

TURBINE

BOILER

Heat loss to stack, turbine, condenser 1,280,000 BTU

0.6 MW output

MHD GENERATION

COAL

545 pounds 6,830,000 BTU

Useful heat 2,045,000 BTU

Overall efficiency **50%**

Coal burning plant improved by magnetohydrodynamics

A major cost to utilities and a growing concern to the public is the placement of high voltage transmission lines carrying power from plants to distribution points. As indicated in Chapter 2, a lot of land is required for transmission rights-of-way. Yet as utilities are forced, in the interest of minimizing air pollution, to put plants farther away from electricity users, more transmission lines are needed.

Until now, telephone, gas and electric companies have, with few exceptions, been unable to work together to develop common rights-of-way or make use of existing public corridors, for example, along highway routes. Sometimes it is simply a question of not being able to decide how to share the construction costs of a common trench. Usually it is because there is no governmental forum—state or federal—in which multiple-use corridors can be worked out. Then there are the myriad planning commissions and zoning boards that must be dealt with at the local level. State energy authorities are going to have to tackle the land-use problems associated with transmission routes. And utilities are going to have to grapple with the economic and technological considerations in placing high voltage lines underground so they will not be unaesthetic nuisances. Better yet, and returning to views we have advanced previously, transmission routing, like plant siting, should be dealt with on a regional basis.

Possible Breakthroughs

Solar energy.   Stop for a moment to consider where all the energy comes from in the first place. What is the primeval as well as the present source? The *sun,* of course. For millennia, it has been radiating energy that has been absorbed and converted in endless ways—to the fuels, currents and natural steam geysers from which man's technological installations have harnessed *power*. We are lucky that the sun's energy was stored in such a useable form. The problem, as has been noted so often in this book, is that the storehouse is not infinite and that burning these products puts their residues into a part of the earth's atmosphere where they are harmful to the environment.

Until now, direct thermal conversion of solar energy to power has been difficult and very expensive on a large scale. The sun diffuses its energy over the entire globe, so that an enormous area is required to capture a sufficient amount of solar energy capable of being converted to useable power. Even so, some U.S. houses have successfully installed solar absorbing devices for heating purposes. Spacecraft and statellites have been using solar energy for quite some time.

But so far, solar energy collectors with a high conversion efficiency have not been developed. It has always been thought that such equipment would be complex and costly, featuring elaborate mirrors, lenses and very special chemicals for coating the absorbing surfaces so that solar heat can be captured and not just reflected or dissipated. Obviously there are also problems in storing solar energy during nighttime and cloudy periods.

Still, it can be done. The question is when? President Nixon in his energy message said that "we expect to give greater attention to solar energy in the future." And he directed the National Aeronautics and Space Administration to accelerate solar energy research. Leon P. Gaucher, a retired scientist from Texaco's Research and Technical Department, wrote in the March, 1971, issue of *Chemtech* that solar energy was not only inevitable but would be necessary to fill the coming power gap. Gaucher did not present much scientific evidence, however. Instead he noted that a major new source of energy has been developed about every thirty years in recent history—coal around 1850, gaseous fuels in the 1870s, liquid fuels in the early 1900s, then hydroelectric and finally nuclear power. Gaucher foresees nuclear fast-breeder generation taking over the bulk of power production in the *coming two centuries* and by 2200, solar energy will have arrived.

There are some men of knowledge and prescience who think that it had better happen long before then. One of these is S. David Freeman who enthuses in apt terms, "The dark horse is the sun. We haven't put our minds to it. The possibilities are both mundane and spectacular." Freeman's staff was impressed with at least one proposal that is receiving serious attention by the government and the National Academy of Sciences. It is a plan, backed with brilliant and thoughtful engineering data, to install in the southwestern California desert a 115-by-115-mile solar absorbing facility that would produce a total of *one million megawatts* and would be able to use its waste heat to make 50 billion gallons of fresh water daily from the ocean—enough water for one hundred and twenty million people. The ecological problems that might occur in the Gulf of California would of course have to be carefully considered. The architects of this plan, Aden B. Meinel and his wife, Marjorie, of the University of Arizona's Optical Sciences Center, feel that environmental safeguards would take care of any adverse side effects (for example, from the disposal of brine) and that the gains in clean power would be well worth the effort.

The Meinels and their colleagues appear to have come up with well-researched new solutions to some of the long-standing technical and economic drawbacks of converting solar energy. They have designed heat-absorbing structures that would minimize heat losses and maximize the capture of high temperature heat. Their system, which seems ideal for so many arid, undeveloped regions of the world—from Death Valley to the Sahara Desert—envisions a network of 1,000 megawatt stations. In a paper, Meinel wrote: "The basic technical capability that is the key to the proposed solution is the ability to make highly selective absorbing coatings. These coatings have high absorbance (black) for sunlight and low emittance (high reflectance) in the infrared . . . We have already made laboratory samples that can reach the operating temperatures needed to operate conventional high pressure steam turbine power generators."

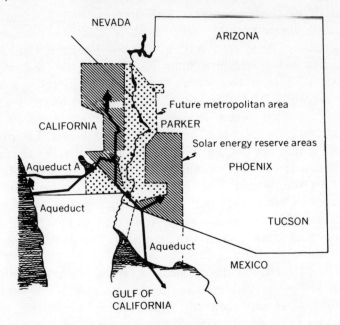

The Meinel's scheme for solar energy

Fusion. Fusion power from thermonuclear reactors is another area in which a breakthrough might be achieved, although it too is far down the road. Such power would incorporate the hydrogen bomb principle. The world's supply of hydrogen is considered to be virtually unlimited. According to the energy staff report just cited, "Controlled fusion has the potential of operating at very high efficiencies and thereby greatly reducing the problem of waste heat disposal . . . In addition, the plant would be inherently safe against a destructive release of energy: it would emit no combustion products to the atmosphere and its reaction products (for *all* cycles) are non-radioactive." A report by the Scientists Institute for Public Information (see Bibliography) agrees with this. Whereas fission, or the splitting of radioactive nuclei, produces troublesome waste products, fusion combines nuclei, such as deuterium, tritium and lithium, and contains or controls the reaction. However, this is simply a theoretical possibility, a principle. It has not to date been actually accomplished and the various experts in and out of government do not see fusion power until the next century, if then.

Fuel cells, geysers, and tides.   In 1971, a Hartford, Connecticut, suburb began to feature home unit fuel cells developed by the Pratt & Whitney division of United Aircraft. Fuel cells were first used in the early 1800s in a crude and experimental fashion. Since then, particularly in the last two decades, this means of providing power has been applied in the aerospace industry in ground transportation systems (e.g. European trains) and in oil pipeline pumping stations. Electricity is produced directly through a chemical reaction. In such a system, hydrogen is usually the fuel that is electrochemically converted to power. Hydrogen comes from any fuel; a main source is natural gas. If coal gasification solves the natural gas shortage, fuel cell power could be widely applied. Environmentally, the process is very clean. However, up to the present, despite the enthusiasm of quite a few companies who are working with fuel cells, this kind of power has been at least three times as expensive as conventional electricity and there have been technical problems as well.

Installations like those in Hartford offer real hope for decentralizing power to a point and reducing the need for new big plants. However, the use of small fuel-cell units ("little black boxes") might in the long-term also produce problems if they become widespread. The impact of producing so many units has to be considered. Also people inevitably would come to demand units large enough to take care of their personal, and perhaps extravagant peak power requirements.

According to a comprehensive survey of the fuel-cell picture in the *Wall Street Journal* (see Bibliography), Atlantic Richfield Company with Bolt, Beranek and Newman, Inc. of Cambridge, Massachusetts, has developed a fuel cell that can run on gasoline, kerosene or propane. At least one power company, Northeast Utilities, and one large manufacturer, Westinghouse Electric Corporation, are enthusiastic about obtaining large-scale fuel-cell plants. However, the success of fuel-cell power will depend on whether natural gas can be extended into the future, on technical and economic problems attendant to large-scale units and on the feasibility of too much decentralization which could become chaotic.

Much of the heat and power needs of Iceland have been provided by natural underground steam geysers. Underground steam apertures in Italy produce some 400,000 kilowatts of power. Pacific Gas and Electric in California produces 82,000 kilowatts from underground steam pressure at a plant about one hundred miles north of San Francisco.

Clearly such energy is restricted to locations where underground reservoirs constantly receive heat from molten matter that is oozing up from beneath the earth's crust. Nobody at this point believes that this so-called geothermal heat will ever be able to produce more than five percent of the world's power. But a little bit will help.

At this stage, tidal power does not loom up as a viable future possibility for solving the energy crisis. But in certain areas, where there is a high rise and drop in saltwater tides, scientists still believe some relief could be obtained by harnessing such great movements of water. For years, both the Canadian and U.S. governments have discussed tidal power projects in the Bay of Fundy and Passamaquoddy Bay. There have been optimistic studies indicating that enough power could be produced to handle more than the requirements of a city the size of Toronto with 2.3 million population. However, like sunlight, the tides are not concentrated. Even so the Nova Scotia government has created an agency (Tidal Power Corporation) and funds ($10 million) for tidal power development.

Buying Time

The trouble with such hoped-for breakthroughs is that a mere pittance has been applied to energy research and development in this country. Billions of dollars have been spent on exploring outer space and ultra-efficient systems of waging war on the land and from the air. Research and development take not only money but *time,* and time is running out. And where the money is really needed, there has been a lot of talk and very little action. Con Ed's Charles Luce has deplored the foot-dragging of his own industry. Instead of the present research and development spending of only $40 million a year, Luce has said for some time "that the level of r & d [research and development] effort for the electric utility industry, exclusive of what the manufacturers do, should be on the order of $200 million to $300 million per year." S. David Freeman agrees. Up to the present time, less than $400 million has been expended by the federal government on energy research, and most of this has been by the AEC on nuclear power. In the report that Freeman directed, *Electric Power and the Environment,* it was noted that research and development expenditures by the utilities amounted to less than one-quarter of one percent of operating revenues. Among the study's conclusions was the recommendation that federal and state regulatory commissions force the utilities to adjust their rates upwards in order to recover far higher research and development expenditures, notably for environmental controls and safeguards. A table containing research and development recommendations is presented below.

TABLE 6: PRIORITY RESEARCH AND DEVELOPMENT TO POWER PLANT SITING

	Estimated FY 1970 federal funding	Estimated FY 1970 non-federal funding	Appropriate magnitude of effort for the future (federal and non-federal)	
			Approximate number of years	Approximate total funding
Waste Treatment and Disposal:				
1. Flue gas treatment to remove SO_2 and NO	$8,300,000	$7,000,000	5 to 10	$150,000,000.
2. Removal of S and noncombustibles from coal before burning	1,100,000	1,000,000	4 to 7	$20,000,000.
3. Low S fossil fuel resource management studies	1,000,000	100,000	4 to 7	$5,000,000.
4. Minimizing NO formation during combustion	430,000	200,000	5 to 8	$5 to $10,000,000.
5. Measurement of submicron flue gas particles	None	None	4 to 7	$1 to $2,000,000.
6. Improved ESP efficiency	250,000	50,000	5 to 10	$10 to $15,000,000.
7. Development of flue gas filters and scrubbers	400,000	100,000	5 to 10	$10 to $15,000,000.
8. Interaction of flue gas with cooling tower plumes	50,000	None	4 to 7	<$1,000,000.
9. Reduction of radioactivity release from nuclear plants	130,000	25,000	2 to 5	$1 to $2,000,000.
10. Collection and disposal of tritium	50,000	25,000	4 to 7	$2,000,000.
11. Prediction of air pollution concentration	1,500,000	100,000	2 to 5	$10,000,000.
12. Decay of air pollutants	350,000	50,000	4 to 7	$1,000,000.
13. Meteorological control through site location	60,000	None	4 to 7	$1 to $2,000,000.
Waste Heat Rejection:				
1. Standardized methods of measuring and correlating water temperatures	None	None	2	$200,000.
2. Heat transfer in water and to atmosphere	1,200,000	None	10 to 15	$10 to $15,000,000.
3. Effects of water temperature on aquatic species	80,000	None	Long-term effort	$5 to $10,000,000 per year.
4. Prediction of water property parameters	155,000	None	5	$500,000.
5. Environmental effects of wet cooling towers	50,000	50,000	3	$300,000.

6. Heat transfer and pressure drop in wet towers	None	Proprietary	3	$300,000.
7. Heat transfer and pressure drop studies for dry towers	None	None	3	$300,000.
8. Operational heat transfer problems of dry towers	None	20,000	3 to 5	$1,000,000.
9. Power plant system studies incorporating dry towers	135,000	10,000	1 to 2	$150,000.
10. Use of dry towers in conjunction with wet cooling systems	None	None	2	$200,000.
11. Use of dry towers in nuclear power plants	None	None	1 to 2	$150,000.
12. Performance of dry towers under various climatic conditions	None	None	1	$100,000.
13. Dry tower demonstration	None	None	3 to 7	$5 to $10,000,000.
14. Process heat and space heating system studies and cost evaluations	150,000	500,000	4 to 7	$1 to $1,500,000.
15. Air conditioning and refrigeration system studies and cost evaluation	50,000	500,000	5	$500,000.
16. Studies of agriculture[1] and aquacultural[2] applications	*100,000	*300,000	4 to 7*	$2,500,000.
	**100,000	**200,000	4 to 7**	$3,000,000.
Underground Transmissions:				
1. Insulation development—Synthetic polymers for EHV cable	None	300,000	2 to 4	$1,000,000.
2. Gas insulated cable development	None	100,000	4 to 7	$3 to $5,000,000.
3. Forced circulation cooling of power cable	None	None	2 to 4	$500,000.
4. Resistive cryogenic cable	12,000 (TVA)	500,000	4 to 7	$5,000,000.
5. Superconducting cryogenic cable	25,000 (BPA)	None	5 to 7	$8,000,000.
6. Testing facility for high power transmission equipment	None	None		$30 to $50,000,000.
Advanced Siting Practices:				
1. Underground siting studies	None	None	2 to 3	$500,000.
2. Offshore siting studies and development	None	None	5 to 10	$10 to $20,000,000.
3. Integrated canal-lake siting studies	None	None	2	$200,000.
4. Energy center siting studies	200,000	50,000	3 to 5	$1 to $2,000,000.

SOURCE: Electric Power and the Environment.

In the end, what it all boils down to is that we must buy as much time as we can through a concerted energy conservation movement while increasing enormously public and private expenditures to try to work a way out of the impasse. There must also be drastic institutional changes, as proposed throughout this chapter, to force large consumers of power to use less and to force the utilities to stop promoting power while they are unable to produce it without severe environmental side effects. As Michael McCloskey, executive director of the Sierra Club, has put it: "Our choice does not need to be one of either blackouts or having the Federal Government tell us to turn off the lights. The more logical course open to us is to turn off the overheated and self-interested forces which are propelling us into a pattern of exponential energy growth."

PART II

TRANSPORTATION

CHAPTER 5

THE MOBILE
AMERICAN

If something so vast and complex as a society can have an
instinct, then one of American society's instincts is for speed,
for getting around, for mobility. And if thwarting a society's
instinct leads to some kind of neurosis, as it often seems to in
individuals, then American society is headed for the madhouse.

In terms of the number of people and the quantity of goods
moved over geographical space, the United States must, as is
claimed, have the "best" transportation system ever seen on
the globe. But tell that to the commuter who is stuck in a traffic
jam every day, or to the factory manager who is waiting well
past the expected arrival date for some vital raw material, or to
the mother waiting at the airport for the return of her daughter
from a transcontinental trip, and they will all turn a few shades
of green and wonder what lobby you are working for. No other
society gives so great an impression of motion as the American
society, and yet it is the common experience of virtually every
American that it is becoming more difficult to get anywhere
from wherever he may be.

Much of the history of the United States is written in terms
of the rapid movement of people and goods from one place to
another—in a succession of transportation modes, in speed.

Or, as historian Daniel J. Boorstin puts it, in *haste*. One of the most romanticized eras of our history is the time when thousands upon thousands of courageous people stripped themselves to the bare essentials, packed those bare essentials into wagons, and set off from one of several booming midwestern towns across the deserts and mountains to settle the Far West. The wagons they used were uncomfortable, light, and inexpensive. They were designed for speed, for the quickest possible trip through dangerous territory. What was left of the wagons after the journey was often simply thrown away or broken up and used for firewood.

Steamboats plying American rivers literally raced. Urged on by passengers who not only wanted to get somewhere fast but who also simply enjoyed the sensation of speed, riverboat captains would pour on the steam, strain the boilers and *make time*. "What had begun as crude necessity," says Boorstin, "ended in dangerous, delightful diversion." It is estimated that of all the steamboats built before 1850, some thirty per cent ended up in accidents.

Americans built clipperships and set records. They built canals which were faster and more economical than bad roads and horse-drawn wagons. And Americans built railroads, almost immediately eclipsing canals, turning these waterways into what most of us now think of as peaceful, quiet places for amateur archaeologists and canoeists to spend silent, slow hours away from the hustle of their daily lives.

When Americans built railroads, they built them to specifications drawn by the American instinct for speed and haste. Our locomotives were much like our prairie wagons. As Boorstein points out in his book *The Americans,* Englishmen built their trains and their roadbeds to last—large, heavy engines that could draw enormous tonnage around long-radius curves at a stately pace. American railroads, on the other hand, were characterized by light engines that also had plenty of power but which did not hold up as well. Roadbeds were built on bad terrain, with steep grades and sharp curves around which the trains would plummet at breakneck speed. Wrecks were common occurrences, but it was the exhilarating sensation of speed that counted, of getting somewhere, of mobility.

This is the context into which American inventors and marketers put the only technological item that can vie for pride of place with Henry Adams' dynamo as the symbol of American life—the automobile. It is in the *idea* of the automobile that the American instincts for speed, mobility—and freedom—reverberate like echoes and amplify themselves. In an automobile, you are your own riverboat captain, your own railroad engineer. *You* press down the accelerator when the historic American urge to *make time* seizes you—with the added advantage that you can choose your own path. You don't have to stick to a river, or to a set of parallel rails: you choose your own way.

Now the automobile has become the context into which all other aspects of American transportation must fit. Against the flexibility and privacy of the automobile, the passenger railroad is a kind of prison, and mass transit in cities is either a planner's dream or a poor man's nightmare. Against the door-to-door efficiency of the trucking industry (one out of every nine American paychecks are connected with the trucking industry according to industry advertisements), the shipment of freight by train, barge, or airplane is pale competition.

The automobile is King. The man behind his own engine is a royal personage. He not only can choose his own road, he even designs them, whether he knows it or not. One of the most respected techniques of the highway planner is wrapped up in the phrase, "desire lines." The technique involves interviewing a number of drivers at an intersection and finding out where they came from and where they are going—point A and point B. That is a desire line. When enough desire lines accumulate—direct lines between point A and point B—someone in some highway department will soon propose a road from A to B, so that drivers will not have to stop at an intersection or take an irritating and time-consuming series of corners.

The only trouble with all of this is that it does not work. These days the kingly driver is caught in a traffic jam on a road that has destroyed the neighborhoods he is looking at through his window, while his mobile castle has become one of the most dangerous polluters of the nation's air. He cannot take a train because it does not run any more. There is obviously no sense in taking the bus since it is stopped ahead of him in the same traffic jam. Moreover, the subways are dirty, unreliable, dangerous or nonexistent. Finally, whatever point B may be, there is little likelihood of finding a parking space there.

It is a familiar litany but not, apparently, familiar enough to make the average American "steamboat captain" think terribly far beyond his own frustration to consider transportation as a system into which he must fit. The reason behind this lack of thought is that transportation is a highly personal matter and any solution to the obvious problems of American transportation must, therefore, take this fact into account or it will certainly, and quite properly, fail.

Lest the point be missed, it may be instructive to dwell a moment on the nature of what is so personal an activity that we hardly ever think of it as "transportation." The word itself comes from the Latin *portare,* to carry, and *trans,* meaning across. To carry implies that *something* is being carried, and across implies that it is being carried *somewhere*—that is, to a destination. But the mobile American has gone far beyond so simple-minded a set of implications. Once given the power to do so, he desires movement for the sake of movement. Consider off-road vehicles such as the dune-buggy, the snow-mobile, the all-terrain vehicle and the other varieties of craft which permit him the ultimate mobility and freedom, that of not having to wait for enough desire lines to accumulate before he takes the direct route from A to . . . where?

One must step very lightly before interfering with such an ingrown desire, so basic an instinct, as the American desire for speed and motion. But perhaps the place to look for solutions is where the instinct reaches its extremes—with the off-road vehicle. The only practical justification for off-road vehicles like the snowmobile is that someone living out in the wilderness may need one to get to a hospital, or less dramatically, a farmer may find them useful in the winter. But such people are few in number and would not support the multi-million dollar business that has mushroomed in the past several years. (There are now over 200,000 dune buggies, 2,000,000 trail bikes, 1,100,000 snowmobiles, and 25,000 all-terrain vehicles in use.) These vehicles have nothing to do with carrying anything vital from one place to any other place. They are, simply, fun; they are a sport.

And, of course, they are dangerous. But so are automobiles and trains and no one has ever seemed to mind this fact very much. However, off-road vehicles are noisy and intrusive; in fact, the scream of the two-cylinder engines is a selling point. Quite ironically, these vehicles are often found in places to which other people travel, by more laborious methods, to get away from the sound of engines among other things. They involve us, as do all forms of transportation, in such questions as land use, and privacy—other people's privacy. It is because such considerations that they are beginning to be banned from various parks, towns, and other public places.

That it is possible, even in a few instances, to tell the mobile American that he cannot use a snowmobile may give some hope and, perhaps, some insight into the business of finding solutions to so personal a problem as transportation. But the less extreme, more common and more important aspects of transportation are also far more complex. And that, in part, is because transportation is so intimately embroiled to where people live.

A good many places where people live today are there because that is where the railroad went. While it is not emphasized in the history books, it is clear that the pattern of settlement west of the early, major centers of the east coast developed largely through the building of railroads. In England, they built railroads to places where people already were, they connected existing settlements with the newest and best mode of transportation. In America, they built railroads to places where they *hoped* people would live. And, indeed, the people moved in and the towns boomed. The towns sold themselves as communities with a future; often they were sold as places where the amenities of life were already to be found.

Indeed, they often were to be found there. In this period of city-building, the supersalesmen who were the town fathers would arrange for a large hotel and a college to be built long before there were enough people to support either. With the help of the railroads, towns grew at fantastic rates and soon became cities like Cincinnati, Chicago, Denver. The growth of these and hundreds of other places in the middle and late 1800s is parallelled only by the remarkable growth of suburbs around these same places since World War II.

The creator of the suburb is, of course, the automobile. Desire lines began to snake out of the cities which the railroads had created. City-dwellers wanted to move out and as more and more people did so, more and larger roads had to be built from the cities into the nearby countryside. With the people went the cities' tax base, leaving behind growing slums—good places to build roads through. Another familiar story which runs tandem with yet another: the rise of the airlines which aggressively sold passenger seats while the railroads withdrew and concentrated on hauling freight. The death knell soon began to sound for all the romantic names—the Twentieth Century Limited, the Californian Zephyr, the Wabash Cannonball and so on—of the inter-city passenger trains, along with the hundreds of far less romantic but useful commuter lines. Eventually, the service got so bad that doctors began to recognize a growing mental disease in Long Island, New York, aptly called the commuter's syndrome.

Total passengers carried by railroads dropped from 1,269,913,000 in 1920, to 285,000,000 in 1970, according to the Interstate Commerce Commission. There will be less, before there is more. When the Federal government took over most of the passenger service in May, 1971, through an organization called Amtrak, it immediately cut the dwindling number of passenger lines to 184. Amtrak also appealed to the airlines, themselves suffering from too many large planes with too many empty seats, for help. In summer 1971, American Airlines was under contract to devise a national, computerized railroad passenger ticketing service.

Meanwhile, the suburbs continue to grow—not really

communities or towns, but places for people with cars to live. They are, in fact, settlements designed by the car for mobile Americans. With the pressure of growing population, and with the negative-feedback of deteriorating cities, the suburbs are growing into cities in their own right. In these growing areas designed by the automobile, one sees the beginnings of a new kind of place to live.

One-half of the new homes built last year rest on wheels. Six million Americans live in mobile homes. These are mostly retired people or working families whose children have grown. They are people who do not wish to live in the old cities with their high crime rates and their terrible public transportation, but who wish for or need a moderately priced home which does not exist in the suburbs. In spite of a number of disadvantages to mobile homes, such as the problem of real estate taxes and the lingering "bad odor" that trailer camps have generally had in the public mind, mobile home parks are growing at an astonishing rate. They are carefully designed with all of the amenities, such as swimming pools, and people are flocking to them in their "double-wides," two 12-by-60-foot units that are towed separately to the site and bolted together. In an article on mobile homes in the *New York Times* Magazine, Douglas E. Kneeland reported that in California alone there are 600 factories producing mobile homes and over 5000 mobile-home parks.

Mobile homes should not be confused with the proliferating varieties of campers which are truly *mobile* second homes and which are jamming up like herds of elephants in state and national parks throughout the country. It costs a great deal to move a mobile home and so most of the new mobile-home parks are permanent communities. It is one thing to slow down your life deliberately, but to be caught in the overall slow-down that is the common exasperation of the mobile American is entirely another thing. The man trapped in his car in a traffic jam may soon realize that as far as transportation is concerned, what began as a delightful diversion has ended up as a crude necessity.

CHAPTER 6

OUR DYING AFFAIR WITH THE CAR

Not long before his death in an airplane crash, Walter Reuther, president of the United Auto Workers, spoke these telling and courageous words about the machine that for so many years had been the lifeblood of his mighty labor force. "I think it is absolutely ridiculous for 100,000 Americans living in the same urban center to try to go to the same place for the same purpose at the same time, as each drives a ton and a half of metal with him. I just think that is utterly stupid from an economic point of view and from a human point of view."

Nothing in American history, perhaps in the entire scope of mankind, has provided as much convenience and joy coupled with frustration and misery as the automobile. Rightly so, it is called the sacred cow of our nation. As already implied in the previous chapter, the car is the ultimate ego trip for the mobility-minded American. It is the essence of technological achievement and supremacy in the hands of the individual. It takes you from the dirty, crowded city neighborhood to the quiet, pastoral countryside. If you don't want to get away from the crowd but would rather just change crowds, you can take your recreational vehicle, your mobile camper, and wheel into a campsite, or park somewhere overlooking a wild river or a

canyon. There is simply nothing like it. The relationship seems
like a love affair but that is only one side of the story, for it is a
union that is becoming less and less enjoyable.

Walter Reuther addressed himself to the automobile's most
visible failure, in the city, where millions of people are caught
each day in traffic jams. He might have added the following
charges or observations.

Poisonous engine emissions and exhaust gases from
automobiles have created a national health hazard, particularly
in cities where these pollutants mount almost every day to a
dramatically dangerous level.

The car has become a debilitating influence on our cash
economy. It is, in itself, an object of misguided veneration.
Even worse, it has created a new consumer culture and a
mobile society, taking people to the shopping center and to
places of work heretofore impossible to consider. The car has
created a life style that has produced an increasing amount of
unhappiness.

The car has been the cause of destructive patterns of land
use. In Los Angeles alone, sixty percent of the land is used for
highways, interchanges, garages, parking lots and service
stations—all to accommodate cars. Public officials and private
contractors conspire with real estate interests wherever and
whenever new roads are to be built, and the result is a wave of
land speculation. Land prices and taxes skyrocket. Poor people
are driven out of their neighborhoods, farmers are taxed off
their lands, and the result is ugly, indiscriminate strip
development, the gasoline alleys that mark America.

Cars give a warped sense of independence and power to the
wrong people. They enable young persons to fly the coop early
and the thrills of driving often lead to tragedy. Nationwide,
automobile accidents account for more deaths than all the wars
in our history, many of them caused by young people in stolen
cars. The car is a major factor of juvenile delinquency, apart
from its role as a vehicle that almost always undermines family
relationships.

The car has become the cornerstone of our gross national
product and we are locked solidly to it with no real alternatives.

When you add up all the industries and interests that relate to the car, you are confronted with a formidable phalanx of economic and political might: the automakers, fuel and fuel additive producers, parts suppliers, motel operations, travel agencies, trucking companies and, not least, the host of road building businesses such as cement, asphalt and aggregate suppliers who arrange lucrative contracts with the highway planners.

In his autobiography, *My Life and Work,* Henry Ford could not have envisioned what would result from the machine that he put on the market and popularized. He was concerned entirely with the virtues of steam propulsion versus the internal combustion gasoline engine. "One of the most remarkable features of the automobile on the farm is the way it has broadened the farmer's life," he wrote. "The obvious thing to do was to design and build a steam engine that would be light enough to run an ordinary wagon or to pull a plow." Ford built such a machine, a steam car fired from a kerosene boiler that had plenty of power. But the big boiler was a psychological menace. To satisfy misgivings about its blowing up, Ford had to make the car too heavy. So after two years of experimenting during the 1870's, he turned to gas power. His first car, a two-cylinder engine model, was built in 1892. According to Ford it "was considered something of a nuisance."

In recent years, many people have mused over what might have resulted if mass auto manufacturers had turned to steam instead of gasoline as the power for cars. Maine Senator Edmund Muskie asked aloud at senate hearings in 1969 how the course of transportation technology would have been changed. There is no clear answer. Possibly steam power would have resulted in larger, more efficient units of conveyance. But in all probability, we would only have a cleaner car and we would still have all the other problems like highways, traffic congestion and the uncontrolled mobility that have wreaked such havoc in our once beautiful land. However, now that highways and parking lots are a *fait accompli,* or until they can be put to more effective use as transportation arteries and terminals, it is imperative that some kind of a clean car be perfected soon.

Effects on Human Health

How has the car become a major health hazard? What are the dimensions of this problem? To begin with, noxious fumes from cars account for sixty percent of the quarter of a billion tons of air pollutants that are dispersed annually throughout the U.S. As a result of the gasoline engine's incomplete or inefficient combustion, we are the victims of hydrocarbon, carbon monoxide, nitrogen oxide and lead emissions. Hydrocarbons are major contributors to smog. Benzo-a-pyrene, the most potent hydrocarbon, is a contributor to cancer. Produced in volume, carbon monoxide is a well-known killer. In small, accumulated doses it is also extremely harmful since it passes without warning into the blood stream and combines with hemoglobin to impede the transportation of oxygen from the lung to the body tissues. Such oxygen deprivation produces a marked slow down in reactions, a loss of visual acuity, nausea and dizziness. The brain is adversely affected and the heart is strained. The danger level of carbon monoxide—ten parts per million for prolonged exposure—is exceeded regularly along congested routes, at strategic intersections and in every metropolis throughout the nation at some point during the day, especially during rush hours and noon. (Often the danger level is exceeded during long periods. In Chicago, for example, the eight hour average was found to be forty-four parts per million.) Oxides of nitrogen interact with hydrocarbons to produce photochemical smog and a by-product, ozone. Both smog and ozone endanger human health. Both cause untold damage to vegetation and crops in agricultural belts such as those of southern California.

The latest member to the list of dangerous pollutants is lead. It has long been labelled a health hazard when present in large doses. Lead-based paints have been a problem for years, but until recently, makers of cars and fuels have dismissed suggestions that lead exhaust traces are dangerous. It would appear, even now, that the main impetus for removing lead additives from gasoline is not based on a concern for human health, but rather because lead inhibits the performance of the new emission controls that will be necessary on all cars in order to meet increasingly stringent Federal Air Quality Standards. Moreover, new evidence shows that lead additives may increase hydrocarbon emissions by causing spark plug fouling and engine misfiring, since they interfere with the oxidation of hydrocarbons in the exhaust system and build up deposits in the engine cylinder.

Until recently, fuel refiners have added an average 2.3 grams of lead per gallon of regular gas (2.7 for premium) in order to reduce engine knock and to protect engine exhaust valves. The total volume of lead additives has been huge—around 500 million pounds a year. About eighty percent has escaped in the exhaust. The World Health Organization has advised that the minimum level of lead ought to be two micrograms per cubic meter in order to protect human health and prevent an interference with essential enzymatic activity within the human metabolism and possible brain damage. This level is well exceeded along every congested artery in the nation, sometimes by as much as twenty times.

Recently it has been found that lead exhaust emissions affect not only human health but, probably, the weather as well. Researchers at the State University of New York at Albany have shown that minute particles of lead will combine with iodine in the atmosphere (put there largely by power plants) to form ideal nuclei around which tiny ice particles can form. Enough of these ice crystals, diffused upward into the clouds, can produce sudden snowfalls and rainstorms—a kind of inadvertant cloud-seeding.

It is all too simple, however, to say that lead should be removed from gasoline immediately. To be sure, automakers are now making engines that can efficiently burn non-leaded gas, but engines produced during the last half decade have depended on lead additives to produce a high enough octane fuel for their high compression ratios. Recent tests and experiments reveal that substitutes for lead additives that will maintain a high enough octane may well result in increased hydrocarbon emissions. At this writing, the matter was not resolved, but most experts agree that lead additives will have to go, since they interfere with the performance of catalytic exhaust control systems being developed to meet new emission standards for nitrogen oxides, hydrocarbons and carbon monoxide. In a comprehensive article on the whole subject (see Bibliography), M. H. Hyman, a California engineer, estimated that lead additives could be removed from fuels by 1973 and that, from a pollution standpoint, satisfactory gasoline could be refined which would cost motorists about ten dollars more per year. In the meantime, owners of older cars can have their engine timing adjusted so that they can use low octane (e.g. 90-91) fuel containing little or no lead additive. (It must be admitted, however, that in some cases, especially for cars with high compression engines, acceleration rates and gas mileage economy will decrease.)

Air Quality

The 1970 Clean Air Act demanded that by 1975 automobile emissions be reduced ninety percent from levels allowed in 1970. On June 30, 1971, William D. Ruckelshaus, administrator of the Environmental Protection Agency, issued the Federal regulations that put teeth in the act. The following table compares emissions, measured in grams per vehicle mile, allowed in 1970 with standards to be met by 1975.

	1970	1975
Hydrocarbons	4.1	0.41
Carbon Monoxide	34.0	3.4

The regulations also set for the first time a standard for nitrogen oxide emissions. They will be limited to 3.0 grams on 1973 car models and 0.4 grams by 1976. At present, cars without nitrogen oxide controls emit 4.0 grams per vehicle mile. *Moreover, under the 1970 Clean Air Act, the procedures by which cars have until now been analyzed for emissions cleanliness have been changed to reflect what actually happens to cars when they are driven by ordinary people, not Detroit engineers.* In the past, Federal Air Quality tests have been performed only on manufacturers' prototypes. Needless to say, these test models have been tinkered with by skilled mechanics and, in some cases, have been allowed to take tests several times after initial shortcomings. It has been shown that out on the road, afterwards, emission controls deteriorate quickly. John B. Heywood, director of MIT's Sloan Automotive Laboratory, reported in a detailed article (see Bibliography) that on the average, emission controls are thirteen percent deficient for carbon monoxide and twenty-five percent deficient for hydrocarbons.

Beginning with the 1972 models, production cars were tested during simulations of a trip of 7.5 miles in a city and after a cold start, that is, after the car had been unused for a period of twelve hours. According to MIT's Heywood, this test was based on the pattern of driving in Los Angeles where temperatures were in the seventies, but it might not work in a chilly climate where it would be necessary to choke the car—and thus enrich the fuel mix—for a cold start.

EPA administrator Ruckelshaus has proposed what he feels is a more equitable procedure to begin with 1975 models. There will be a cold start test and then a hot start analysis when the engine has been turned off for ten minutes following the first run. The results will be combined and weighted to reflect forty-three percent of the cold start emissions, and fifty-seven percent of the hot start.

In the summer of 1971, environmental officials in New Jersey, the most densely populated state in the nation and one with the highest amount of highway traffic, announced a comprehensive automobile inspection program to begin in 1972. *All* of the 3.3 million cars registered in the state will undergo a test of emissions. With the help of a federal grant for trying out the testing procedure, New Jersey's Department of

Environmental Protection will inaugurate a thirty-second emissions inspection by machine, part of the usual safety inspection. The following standards, reported in the *New York Times*, will be used in the test.

Cars made in	Carbon Monoxide	Hydrocarbons (parts per million)
1967 or before	7.5%	1200
1968-1969	5%	600
1970 or later	4%	400

Visible smoke will mean automatic failure; and the standards will be stiffened further in 1973. Failure will mean the owner has two weeks to spend the twenty dollars or so needed to reduce emissions to these levels or he must keep the car off the road. New Jersey officials estimate that this will reduce the state's load of auto-produced carbon monoxide by twenty percent in the first year, and hydrocarbons by thirty-two percent.

In another antipollution effort, the City of Philadelphia began in August, 1971, to enforce a 1954 ordinance forbidding visible smoke in the exhausts of autos, trucks and buses.

It is not within the scope of this chapter to debate whether EPA has been aggressive enough in applying the conditions of the Clean Air Act or whether loopholes will soon be found in federal or state testing procedures and other areas. Come what may, the regulations will be tough to meet. The Ford Motor Co.'s executive vice president, L. A. Iacocca, decried the Clean Air bill just before it emerged from the Congressional drawing boards. He complained that "unless the science and technology of emission control move ahead much faster than we believe is possible, we will not be able to meet the standards prescribed by the bill."

The authors of this book charge that Detroit is playing the same old game of procrastination, trying to buy time while figuring out how best to meet the inevitable—an automobile with *zero* emissions, undoubtedly an alternative to the internal combustion engine, and a balanced national transportation system that includes a number of other conveyances besides the cars, such as rapid transit. It is notable that when terrible smog first appeared over Los Angeles in the 1940s, auto industry spokesmen declared authoritatively that this condition was meteorologically and otherwise unique to southern California. Of course they were wildly wrong. Then when that state imposed the first tough emission control standards, the industry wailed that pollution controls would not be technologically possible in time. When "outsiders" developed such controls, the big manufacturers in Detroit quickly came up with an effective system. In New Jersey, having had the new testing procedures imposed, representatives of the auto manufacturers could only endorse the program. Indeed, such impositions may continue from many quarters. In August, 1971, a U.S. Court of Appeals in Washington, D.C., ruled that the health and environmental hazards of autos were much like those of cigarettes, and ordered the Federal Communications Commission to assure that network programming included warnings of these hazards while the manufacturers extol the performance of their products.

After the EPA issued regulations in 1971, the lament continued. Indeed, there are some real obstacles to overcome. One is the fact that present means of controlling carbon monoxide and hydrocarbon emissions result in as much as a fifty percent increase in nitrogen oxides. Yet, Federal air quality officials think the standards can be met with recirculating devices for nitrogen oxides, changes in fuel and the combustion stage, with new fuel injection systems and with space age exhaust systems featuring, for example, thermal reactors made of extremely heat resistant metal to replace manifolds.

In his analysis of the situation, MIT's Heywood speculated that the following changes would occur. 1) Hydrocarbon and carbon monoxide emissions would be reduced by enabling the engine to operate on a lean fuel mix. 2) Afterburner type devices in the exhaust system would handle unburned pollutants. Such devices might be thermal reactors on the engine head or catalytic reactors beneath the car. 3) Nitrogen oxide reduction would be accomplished by combustion and timing adjustments as well as by a recycling mechanism that would insert cooled exhaust gas back into the air intakes resulting in a lower flame temperature. In any event, Heywood foresees a more expensive and less economic internal combustion engine.

If that is the result, a market should develop for a different kind of engine. Certainly the growing costs of automobile operation ought to be an incentive to reducing our dependence on cars and the number of cars we buy. For when you consider depreciation, the costs of parking and the pains endured in using a car to commute, it cannot be considered much of a return on your investment.

Future Cars

What are the alternatives to the internal combustion or gasoline powered car? The answer to that question is speculative. And before venturing at it, the authors want to make one point very clear. *It would be misguided and even tragic if our search for a new car overlooked the dire need to reduce the number of automobiles—even if they are clean—driven by anyone in the U.S. who can pass a driving test. The automobiles that surely will be developed must fit into a national transportation plan which will set guidelines for getting about within the city, between cities, between cities and suburbs and over the long stretches of sparsely developed country.* Laws, excise and other taxes, high operating costs and the expenses of pollution control should make the car an object of necessity only, a means of conveyance to serve where nothing else will. This may seem like heavy medicine, for just about all of us have become dependent upon cars. Even when public transportation is available, we avoid it because seldom is it tailored precisely to our inclinations and whims. In a nation where planning and predictability are dismissed in favor of flexibility and sudden maneuverability, the car represents the ultimate means of escape.

It would seem that we are about ready to go back to Henry Ford's steam car. By mid-1971, the Environmental Protection Agency had awarded development contracts to at least three companies. One of these, Steam Engine Systems, had come up with a pilot model one hundred horsepower steam engine. Previously, a Senate Commerce Committee studied alternatives and in a report titled *The Search for A Low-Emission Vehicle* advocated accelerated federal support for the Rankine Cycle steam principle engine. It is so-called because it does not depend on water for steam, which would present a freezing problem in many parts of the nation. In the Rankine cycle, steam vapor heated in a coil (not one of Henry Ford's big boilers) drives pistons or turbines. Heat is not provided by an inefficient series of explosions as is the case with internal combustion, but by a steady *external* flame which burns cleanly and slowly at atmospheric pressure. Fuel could be low-grade gas or kerosene. The latter is favored at present.

Experimental cars featuring the Rankine cycle have proven clean enough to satisfy foreseeable air quality standards. The Senate Commerce Committee report concluded flatly that "the Rankine Cycle Propulsion System is a satisfactory alternative to the present internal combustion engine in terms of performance and a far superior engine in terms of emissions."

The trouble with all this is that Detroit, as yet, has too much at stake in gasoline internal combustion cars to have devoted more than token effort toward an alternative. The biggest portion of industry capital investment has been in annual styling changes and advertising—a figure in excess of one billion dollars. Those who have supported the alternatives have been concertedly discredited or ignored. One such person is William P. Lear, the very clever inventor of the first car radio, the executive jet, the auto-pilot for jet planes and numerous other marvelous devices. Lear's explorations have taken many twists and turns. At the end of 1970, having once given up on a steam car, he produced a 22-pound steam-vapor turbine that he claimed would be pollution-free, cheaper in costs and operating economics and longer lasting than any car engine yet built.

As this book was written, it appeared that sooner or later,

with or without Detroit's compliance, a steam car would be developed. Size and weight limitations would be overcome and the Lears of this world would be vindicated.

There were other alternatives as well. For about $350, a gasoline engine can be modified to take natural gas. But this will only be feasible with fleets of cars such as taxicabs or government vehicles, since the cruising range is limited and it is most convenient to have a central servicing station. As noted in the energy section of this book, the supply of natural gas is also limited.

Both Ford and General Motors have been working on gas turbine engines. However, so far, various complications have limited these units to heavy vehicles such as buses and trucks. Moreover, nitrogen oxide emissions have remained high because the gas turbine engine burns fuel continuously at an extremely high temperature—1,500 degrees and higher. Many experts hold out hope for gas turbine cars in the distant future, but they are expensive to build and the high combustion temperatures present real, perhaps insurmountable problems.

There has been talk about hybrid cars. One example did extremely well in an MIT-sponsored "Clean Car" race across the country and would probably have won if it had not suffered an unusual breakdown. It depended on power from electric batteries that were charged from a generator driven by external combustion.

Late in the fall of 1970, General Motors paid $50 million for the rights to the Wankel Rotary Engine, heretofore a dirty means of propulsion but operating on a principle allowing for much improvement in controlling emissions. The ever ingenious and competitive Japanese have also come up with a rotary engine car, the Marda, that as of this writing had not been proven in the U.S., even though its makers, Toyo Kogyo, claimed that the small car could run cleanly and efficiently on low octane fuel and would meet tougher U.S. air quality standards.

One other development aroused some interest among auto industry observers: In the spring of 1971, General Motors hired Prof. Ernest S. Starkman as vice-president in charge of environmental affairs. *Saturday Review* science editor John Lear noted perceptively that Starkman, as a professor of mechanical engineering at Berkeley and an advisor to the California Air Resources Board, had been on a panel that had stated the following in a March, 1970 report to the White House Office of Science and Technology: "In spite of intensive industry efforts, there is a probability that the gasoline piston engine will not be clean enough to meet long term air quality requirements. This probability is sufficiently high to warrant serious attention to alternative power plants." When contacted by Lear, Starkman remained consistent. Gas turbine engines would be the earliest solution, he felt, while eventually cars would be powered from some kind of batteries or fuel cells. The point is that even if internal combustion engines can meet 1975 air quality standards, the number of cars on the road is projected to increase so much that the total emissions, on a nationwide basis, will go up again. Alternative power must be found and, in any case, the number of cars stabilized. Automobile congestion and the incredible amount of land taken up for roads make this imperative.

Roads To Ruin

The highways that cars need have despoiled and dehumanized America. Despoilment has come with the laying of asphalt, aggregate and concrete on the best land, the rending apart of countryside and small towns, the dividing of close neighborhoods in cities and the use of waterfront that should have become a public trust and opportunity instead of an ugly strip of roadway. Dehumanization has come as road systems have introduced homogeneity and standardization into a realm where once there was splendid diversity and localism. On the old roads, improved paths that had been found vital for communication by both the Indian and the pioneer, you could tell just where you were in America. You moved along with the contours of the land, and the local inn possessed the peculiar flavor and style of the region. Now, as novelist David Rounds wrote about a sightseeing trip, "the dominant tourist facilities are the motel and roadside restaurant, which even when they are not part of a chain look like the links of one." Rounds tried his best to observe by car the character of New York's North Country, but he found that he was closed off from the landscape. "The modern road," he wrote in an article for the *New York Sunday Times*, June 20, 1971, "is so built up from and fenced off from the terrain it has gouged out during its construction that to travel it is hardly to experience the landscape at all since one is undergoing almost none of the land's conditions; one is simply experiencing the road. The ultimate modern road is the superhighway, which entirely subdues the terrain and precisely by doing so becomes throughout its course entirely uniform, so that the motorist so inclined can follow it for a thousand miles without having, in any real sense, gone anywhere at all." So goes one man's lament about highways.

The modern road system that crisscrosses the U.S. land and city scape did not really take shape until right after the Second World War when the number of cars on the road zoomed upwards, from 25 million in 1945 to 40 million by 1950. During this period, federal aid programs for highway construction established precedents in public works largess that, at this writing, have continued to resist the challenges of honest citizen-activists and reform-minded members of government. The capping stone was the creation by Congress in 1956 of the Highway Trust Fund to provide continuing revenues for the Interstate Highway System.

This trust fund claims just over seventy percent of the taxes paid on gasoline, motor vehicles, tires and other automotive equipment. In the last several years, trust fund revenues have run upwards of five billion dollars. The money is appropriated for federal road grants to the interstate system's primary and secondary roads. The states are given ninety percent of the money spent on interstate roads. For the other types the grants vary from fifty to seventy-five percent. *It is no wonder that state politicians scramble to contrive roads for such handouts.* In a first-rate piece of reporting for the *Washington Monthly* (see Bibliography), David Hapgood wrote that "nothing generates more financial return, legal or otherwise, to those in office than highway construction money, and it is unlikely that any official who wants to stay in Washington will put too many obstacles in the path of that money to the states."

One of the original reasons for the interstate system of highways appears ludicrous in the light of history. It was the rationale applied over the years to so many other boondoggle programs—national security. The idea is to make those who object look unpatriotic. Indeed, it was argued hotly when the system was created in 1944 that there was an urgent need for modern highways over which troops could be moved to defend the nation in time of a crisis. The interstate network was also expressly designed to provide fast links between cities and states for long-haul traffic and trucking. In actuality the interstate system has been mangled by the politicians so that it includes more than 5,000 miles of arteries *within* cities and has been accused by countless experts of being a major contributor to urban congestion. The bypass has become an impasse.

In 1956, when the interstate system was given a regular flow of money, its projected cost was $27 billion for 41,000 miles of road. Since then, about two-thirds of the system has been completed at a cost of some $40 billion. Total mileage has been increased to 42,500, and the most recent projected costs are $69.9 billion.

It is doubtful that the network will be completed by 1975, four years beyond its deadline, if at all. The trust fund which was to have expired in September, 1972, has been extended by Congress through October, 1973. Moreover, the mighty highway lobby and its pals on Capitol Hill already are plotting a new road system for rural America that will replace the interstate network and require a regular flow of money like the trust fund. The justification for this system will undoubtedly be "economic development" for deprived and isolated areas. It is no wonder that the highway lobbyists acquiesced when the federal government took over the management of major urban railroads with the Railpax Corporation. *This move eliminated or severely hurt the local rail carriers that served rural towns, opening the way for new road service.* When trucking and highway interests get together, the advocates of balanced transportation take it on the chin.

Federal government handouts are not the only means for supporting modern road construction. In 1970, a total of some $20 billion was spent on roads. Highway-related jobs supported fifteen percent of the nation's work force. State taxes, as well as federal, poured into the public works coffers. Clearly such a public works policy is a monstrous drain on the U.S. taxpayer. It dictates a dependency on automotive travel that is inefficient and frustrating and against the will, or beyond the choice, of a great many people. How can it continue? The answer is simple. The highway lobby is second only to the military-industrial complex in its political clout. Helen Leavitt in her painstakingly thorough book, *Superhighway—Superhoax* (see Bibliography) wrote the following: "The continuing momentum for the highway program is provided by a staggering number of private interests. The average motorist is unaware of some of these organizations because many are closed clubs, although they testify before congressional road committees whose purpose it is to determine how many highways the public is supposed to need each year. Many public officials whose duty it is to protect the public are themselves members of these closed clubs."

When the American Association of State Highway Officials says that Congress should spend $285 billion on roads in the decade beginning in 1975, it can count on plenty of support. The host of organizations lobbying for road projects needs a directory. The American Road Builders Association represents over 5,000 contractors, materials suppliers, makers and sellers of construction equipment, engineers, banking and real estate speculators, government officials and even members of Congress. Jennings Randolph, Senate Public Works committee chairman, was once ARBA treasurer. Congressman George Fallon, chairman of the House Public Works committee before he was defeated in 1970, largely as a result of opposition from the League of Conservation Voters, was an honorary member of the highest standing. Fallon was chief architect of the Highway Trust Fund. Other important organizations waving the flag for roads include the Associated General Contractors of America, the National Highway Users Conference, the American Trucking Association, The Automotive Safety Foundation, the Highway Research Board and the Automobile Manufacturers Association. Mrs. Leavitt provides the following chart in her book, showing the organizational ties of the so-called highwaymen.

INTERLOCKING ORGANIZATIONS
THROUGH DUAL MEMBERSHIP OR JOINT COMMITTEES

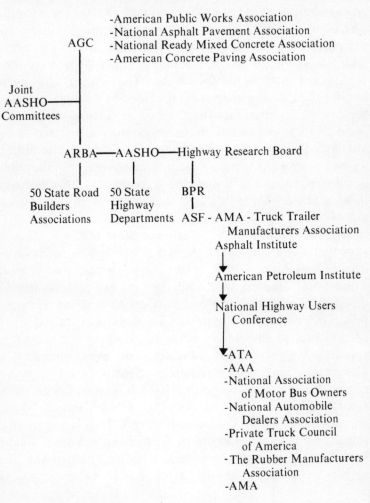

AGC
-American Public Works Association
-National Asphalt Pavement Association
-National Ready Mixed Concrete Association
-American Concrete Paving Association

Joint AASHO Committees

ARBA——AASHO——Highway Research Board

50 State Road Builders Associations

50 State Highway Departments

BPR

ASF - AMA - Truck Trailer Manufacturers Association
Asphalt Institute

American Petroleum Institute

National Highway Users Conference

-ATA
-AAA
-National Association of Motor Bus Owners
-National Automobile Dealers Association
-Private Truck Council of America
- The Rubber Manufacturers Association
-AMA

In both the city and the country, highways receive support not only from the directly related interests just cited but also from land speculators. It has often been said, and often proven through investigative reporting and occasional court hearings, that those who would exploit the property in the path and along the route of planned highways are the main proponents of new roads. In the following chapter this will be made quite apparent. It is certainly obvious when you look about you or question taxpayers along the highways. Poor land skyrockets in value when it is a potential motel site. Public officials who are privy to road plans often turn up as property owners enriched greatly by the projects.

The Highway Revolt

Who has been foolish enough to array themselves against the *highwaymen?* What are their weapons? What are their chances?

The revolt began, and to a large extent continues, as a guerrilla uprising on the part of people who were being individually uprooted or saw their neighborhoods being divided by roads. Thus, it began in the cities. It is a strife that will be discussed in detail in the next chapter. In general, people began to look around them and saw how the landscape was being covered by concrete strips, cloverleafs and the ancillary parking spaces. They saw the ugliness and impersonality spawned by these roads. They saw their personal privacy being invaded not only by the sounds of traffic but by the hordes of people that moved like lemmings down these new roads.

One of the authors was saddened by the sight he saw when he emerged from a canoe trip in the Maine woods in the summer of 1971. The state campsite by scenic Whetstone Falls had been taken over by motor-campers, not in cars but in huge recreational vehicles that were totally equipped with the comforts of home, butane stoves, refrigerators and even generating capacity to handle small television sets. These enormous mobile monsters had created a hopeless traffic jam in a small forest clearing that had originally been provided for those who loved the woods and the austerity which "roughing it" traditionally required when camping. How had this happened? For the most part, the scene described above is the result of the number of roads that were constantly being opened in this wilderness. Forest paths became dirt tracks and the tracks were paved over for country roads and the country roads were widened into highways. Soon this area in the Maine woods was no longer what it once was.

The 1968 Federal Highway Act gave the public a new opportunity to participate in the early stages of highway planning by providing that there be *two* public hearings held regarding highway plans. One hearing would discuss the general corridor for the road and the other would cover design features and the precise location. Of course, we are only talking here about highways built with federal matching money. Unfortunately for the public, a stronger proposal fell by the political wayside. It would have required hearings to "explore the question of whether alternative modes of transportation would better serve the public interest."

In actual fact, federal highway administrators have not aggressively, if at all, carried out their mandate to involve the public *except in those instances where intense heat has been generated by indignant individuals and citizen action groups.*

For a moment, there was a real mood of change and a new commitment to balanced transportation within the Federal Department of Transportation. J. Dorm Braman, former mayor of Seattle and now a former DOT assistant secretary for environment and urban systems, said time and time again that transportation "should be one of the means for reaching community objectives. If the objectives are not readily apparent, then the transportation process should be a medium for stimulating communities to join in formulating goals before making a substantial commitment to any transportation component. Elected officials," Braman would emphasize, "should be given real policy choices, not engineering choices." He was joined by Oscar Gray, a former director of DOT's Office of Environmental Impact, who publicly bemoaned the failure of state highway departments to cooperate, much less communicate, with regional and state planning agencies.

Since then, the Department of Transportation has responded positively to several highway planning *crises* but it has failed to implement the policy imperatives of men like Braman and Gray that highway planning must leap far beyond a discussion of road systems and consider 1) whether the roads are needed in the first place, 2) what other types of transportation might serve better and 3) how will various systems of travel complement existing modes and affect the lives of people in a particular region.

In the meantime, the revolt has gained a measure of political support. State governors like Massachusetts' Francis Sargent and city mayors like New York's John Lindsay have taken up the cry that federal road grants should be used at the discretion of local officials for transportation systems that are needed most urgently by a particular state or community. In smogbound California, citizens succeeded in putting on the 1970 general election ballot a proposition to enable state and federal gas and road taxes to be used for pollution studies and rapid transit. The highwaymen went into a high-gear counterattack to have the measure defeated. The available evidence indicates they may have spent one million or more dollars compared to the approximately $20,000 spent by environmental proponents. Contractors, oil companies, car dealers, cement firms, truckers, automobile clubs and tire companies joined forces and brought off victory, 3.1 million votes to 2.7 million, not a substantial margin.

Maryland is one state that has taken positive steps to overcome the highway syndrome, although it remains to be seen what will happen in the long run. A state department of transportation was created in 1970 and mandated with responsibility "for the development and maintenance of a continuing, comprehensive and integrated transportation planning process . . . ." Most important, the department can make discretionary use of highway taxes. In the U.S. Congress, there are also pending proposals to free Highway Trust Fund monies for urban mass transit and balanced public transportation systems.

Until there are new laws that are strictly enforced, citizens must resort to legal action in order to stop those highways that clearly appear to be a waste of taxpayers money and a definite environmental intrusion. In this sector of the battle, there have been some notable successes.

Conservationists opposed plans to build an 18.5 mile section of interstate highway in Franconia Notch, New Hampshire just beneath the Old Man of the Mountain, a peak of considerable beauty. On grounds that the road would mar the region, John Volpe, secretary of transportation, postponed indefinitely the granting of federal aid for building it.

A more important victory was won over plans to build a section of interstate highway through Overton Park, a 342-acre public woods in downtown Memphis, Tenn. DOT went ahead and approved construction of the road with federal funds. Citizens To Preserve Overton Park, Inc. contended in a court suit to stop the road that it was unlawful under the Department of Transportation Act and Federal Aid Highway Act to build a road through a public park unless there was "no feasible and prudent alternative." They also charged that DOT had withheld the factual data on which it had made its approval decision. In March, 1971, the U.S. Supreme Court ruled against the federal government and ordered a district court to conduct a "thorough, probing, in-depth review" of the Overton Park plans.

At this writing, it was not yet clear how various environmental provisions in federal statutes, including the National Environmental Protection Act itself, would affect highway planning. These can be interpreted liberally by the administrators of federal highway aid. Once they have considered the alternatives to a planned road, the effect it might have upon the environment and upon people, they can still arbitrarily decide that the highway funds will be granted.

A far tougher, far more enlightened mandate is needed for transportation planning to become sensible and humane as well as part of the overall community planning process. What is *not* needed is another bill to reestablish the Highway Trust Fund for another fifteen years.

CHAPTER 7

THE URBAN
IMPASSE

During the morning rush hour of June 24, 1969, President Richard M. Nixon hovered in a helicopter over the highway approaches to Washington, D.C. As he watched the slow crawl of traffic, the president is reported to have remarked to his escort, John Volpe, secretary of transportation, "I sure am glad I don't have to drive to work."

Despite this observation, the president was apparently not enlightened much by the trip. A short while later, his administration made a deal with pro-freeway Congressmen that would entangle the District of Columbia still further in a knot of traffic and would vastly reduce the chances for rapid transit and other alternative modes of transportation in Washington, D.C.

The Nation's Capital: A Model Nightmare

What has happened in the nation's capital is a classic example of bad transportation planning. The present plans for the District of Columbia are against the will of a majority of the citizens as expressed through their representatives in government and are clearly dictated in the interests of those who live in Virginia and Maryland suburbs. In other words, suburban interests are calling important shots in urban government, an absurd development that prevails throughout the U.S.

Furthermore, once implemented, the transportation "plans" for Washington will certainly boomerang, and automobile commuters will find themselves in a worse mess than ever before. In addition, these plans are in clear violation of the intent of federal highway legislation, if not an actual contradiction of the letter of the law. This matter is presently in the hands of the courts.

Russell E. Train, chairman of the president's Council for Environmental Quality, was saddened by what he saw was happening. Then head of the Conservation Foundation, he wrote a personal letter to President Lyndon Johnson dated August 2, 1968, urging a veto of the 1968 Highway Act which resulted in the District's becoming a victim of the highway lobby. Train wrote, "The bill's directives for District of Colombia freeways would set a national precedent that violates the central purpose for which the Department of Transportation was created: to replace an urban transportation system dominated by the automobile with balanced systems using a variety of methods of transportation." He commented further that, "The bill would deny civic rights inherent in a democracy."

What did this 1968 Highway Act do? It ordered the District immediately to build a major bridge across the Potomac River and three highway segments totalling about thirty miles. How can a national act do this, particularly when the local government has rejected these roads? That is the question and it has not yet been given proper consideration by those with the power to do something about it. Moreover, a state of bondage has been created that had, at the time of this writing, stirred up a hostile and ominous revolt among the urban citizenry.

Just over a year after the Highway Trust Fund was established in the 1950's to subsidize the Interstate Highway System, the District of Columbia Highway Department went to "the trough," as the Highway Trust Fund is called, with ambitious plans for interstate segments within the city and on its approaches. Meanwhile, plans were also made for a rapid transit system. In July, 1960, the House and Senate District Committees issued a report concluding that "any attempt to meet the area's transportation needs by highways and private automobiles alone will wreck the city."

The prestigious consulting firm of Arthur D. Little, Inc. reviewed the District's transportation plans in 1966 and issued a report that scored existing freeway proposals for the city. District highway planners were criticized for basing their requests on insufficient data and outmoded transportation projection techniques, as well as failing entirely to give proper consideration to the social and environmental impact of highway systems.

In spite of such advice, the highway planners continued to receive support from the U.S. Congressional committee that virtually can throttle the District through control of its budget. The only concession was a change in plans for the North Central Freeway, a road designed to provide a new avenue to the city for white suburbanites in Maryland. Whereas the traffic planners had originally favored a route along Wisconsin Avenue, beginning in Georgetown, the city's most expensive real estate, and running out through white residential enclaves, the freeway was shifted over to northeastern Washington through black and integrated residential neighborhoods. As David Hapgood so rightly observed in his previously cited article for *Washington Monthly,* "This is basic highway strategy: go where the clout is least. 'Through the park or ghetto' is the urban highway planner's slogan. In Washington," Hapgood noted, "they tried both. North Central was at one time routed through Rock Creek Park."

With this, various citizens' groups that previously had fought only for their own narrow objectives joined together to form the Emergency Committee On The Transportation Crisis. This citizen organization has been concerned mainly with the North Central Freeway, but it has also opposed the Three Sisters

Bridge which would cross the Potomac River at the north end of the Georgetown district and eventually join up with the freeway.

Accurately calling the North Central "a white man's highway through black men's bedrooms," whites and blacks together went to work to convince the U.S. Congress and the federal government that the citizens of the District did not want a new bridge and three more interstate segments. Alan Boyd, then secretary of transportation, agreed that the Three Sisters Bridge would only move Virginia's traffic congestion across the river and into the District. The highway revolt gained some new momentum. On February 15, 1968, the U.S. Court of Appeals, in response to a citizens' suit, issued an injunction against construction of all the controversial road projects until the District Highway Department had complied with laws requiring public hearings on such highway proposals.

The highway lobby wasted no time in working on the House of Representatives District Committee and having a section tacked onto the 1968 Federal Highway Act that ordered the District to complete its interstate links (the Three Sisters Bridge, North Central Freeway and two legs of an inner loop system), *"notwithstanding any other provision of law, or any court decision or administrative action to the contrary."*

When the Highway Act was in the hands of President Johnson for signing, Russell Train and other environmentalists urged a veto. If the bill containing the District of Columbia proviso were enacted, they said, dangerous precedents would be established. For one thing, the House of Representatives would seize the power to act similarly regarding highway plans throughout the nation. For another, the bill would henceforth allow highway planners to flaunt public participation and public wishes.

Train's letter was cogent and persuasive and, because of his influence within the administration today, is well worth quoting: "The bill would require the District of Columbia to accept a single-element transportation system that ignores not only District plans but the recommendations of the Department of Transportation. That Department recognizes that our large cities suffer increasingly from traffic congestion and air pollution. In Washington congestion is severe, and the automobile the greatest single air polluter. The city must therefore develop a transportation system that will include mass transit. But construction of the proposed Potomac River Expressway, the Three Sisters Bridge, the center and east legs of the Inner loop, and the mandate for future expressway links would effectively eliminate many future options of the city to develop a balanced system . . . . With primitive arrogance, the narrowest engineering concepts applying to a local situation have been attached to a national bill of a very different import. The country can no longer afford, and the nation's capital certainly does not deserve, a highway bill that so denies vital environmental and social concepts."

But President Johnson signed the bill, though he issued the accompanying statement that he felt that the federal government could, at its own discretion, disregard Section 23, the mandate to the District. The president also urged the District City Council and the National Capital Planning Commission, a citizens' advisory board with no real authority, to revise the comprehensive transportation plan for the District. This was done and a compromise plan was presented that did not include the Three Sisters Bridge and much of the other controversial links.

At this point, a new villain entered the confrontation. He was William H. Natcher, chairman of the District Appropriations Subcommittee and a true friend of the highwaymen. Natcher had a big club—namely the $1.1 billion in federal matching appropriations for a District of Columbia rapid transit subway system. (Maryland and Virginia voters had approved a $500 million bond issue to go with the federal money.) Natcher said his committee would not release an initial appropriation of $34.2 million for the subway unless the interstate highway segments were built immediately.

As this book was written, in the summer of 1971, the whole matter was unresolved. The administration had cooperated with Natcher and joined the House in putting pressure on the District Council to overturn its previous ruling against the highways. Yet another court order, this time responding to an *amicus curiae* brief of conservation organizations and citizens, halted construction on the Three Sisters Bridge.

Byron Kennard, transportation chairman for the Audubon Naturalist Society of the Central Atlantic States and a staff member of the Conservation Foundation, vainly initiated an appeal to Train to have the National Environmental Protection Act applied to the District situation. Kennard and others, including the Metropolitan Washington Coalition for Clean Air, felt that federal aid should not be granted to projects that might result in increased violations of the Federal Air Quality Act (e.g. pollution from cars) as well as federal statutes relating to parkland in the Capital area and along the river where the bridge would be built. In point of fact, NEPA Section 102 requires environmental statements from federal agencies whenever the federal government is involved in a project that might affect the environment in a significant manner. Since that act became a law, no such statements have been filed concerning the District interstate segments or, for that matter, countless other federally subsidized highways.

While Washington, D.C.'s Mayor Walter Washington has opposed the North Central Freeway, his highway director Thomas F. Airis has insisted that the controversial highway segments, most notably the North Central Freeway, are urgently needed. The conflict has been made infinitely more complex by several other developments. One was the 1970 Federal Highway Act's requirement that the route selection for the North Central Freeway and Inner Loop links be carefully restudied. In May, 1971, Congressman Natcher announced that his committee would release appropriations for the rapid transit system—the $34.2 million for 1971 plus $38.1 million for 1972—because the administration had agreed to comply with both the 1968 and 1970 Highway Acts. Presumably this meant that the administration would ask the U.S. District Court to lift its injunction against construction work on the Three Sisters Bridge and would award a contract immediately for restudying routes of the North Central Freeway and loop segments.

Then in the summer of 1971, *Washington Post* reporter, Jack Eisen, uncovered a private arrangement—not since denied—between the federal government and Mr. Natcher that would seal the bargain to release the rapid transit funds. On the part of the federal government, the *Post* reported that Interior Secretary Rogers Morton and DOT Secretary Volpe had agreed to go ahead with plans for a six-lane interstate highway that would go past and under major national shrines to link the Three Sisters and Theodore Roosevelt Bridges with the Southwest Freeway, thus bringing heavy truck traffic right under the Lincoln Memorial. Apart from degrading the grounds by the Lincoln Memorial, Tidal Basin and Jefferson Memorial, this highway would cut through a twenty-seven-acre site planned for a memorial to President Franklin D. Roosevelt.

The highwaymen have spun such a web of freeways around Washington that few people can comprehend what is going on. Moreover, as Hapgood noted in his article in 1969, "A reservoir of anti-highway opinion exists among residents of threatened neighborhoods, conservationists, planners, and most recently, environmental scientists; but up until now, nobody has tried to bring these dissidents together as a national pressure group."

Yet the Washington revolt has succeeded in galvanizing different opposing factions to an unprecedented degree and out of this crisis may yet come victory and a dramatic change in the national climate.

Mrs. Angela Rooney, an articulate and active participant in Washington's ECTC, summed up in very moving terms the way in which the highwaymen have wielded power and the way in which urban dwellers are made to feel totally without power, pawns in the hands of those who feel that cities are beyond hope as places to live and simply have become service centers for the suburbs. "Mobility is a basic right," she told one of the authors, "but the highway lobby has deprived us of that right. This situation is compounded in the District of Columbia where there is no strong representative government but instead a District Committee which has become a political trading stamp for the Congressmen that sit on it. The white suburban districts hold the political edge. The planners increasingly view the city with contempt. Poor people are bullied into giving up their property without a fight. They are told that there is no money for their relocation or that they will be paid less than fair market value if they don't comply. Residential areas are purposefully blighted as they are held indefinitely under the threat of condemnation for a highway. All the time the commercial real estate interests make money off speculation. You have a mobile society that is easily manipulated and it doesn't make sense. It is just silly to build a highway system to take people back and forth in circles thirty miles around the city or into the city to get to work every day. Instead, we've got to encourage a system under which people will live, work and die in the same place where they were born."

The Pattern

The transportation crisis of Washington, D.C. aptly enough is a reflection of a national condition, a microcosm of an impasse that has tied up virtually every large city in the United States. The capital's woes are cut to a standard pattern.

Roads carrying fast and noisy traffic rip cities asunder, making them less desirable places to live. It was one thing when roads were built for carriages and other horse-drawn conveyances. A modern highway requires a corridor many times wider, and a city interchange linking several interstate roads uses up to 150 acres of land. It has been estimated that every car that enters a city on an average workday demands 300 square feet for parking and maneuvering into a parking spot. Highways take up room, destroy old neighborhoods and use up valuable open space. Quite clearly, they are a major factor in making cities less enjoyable places to live.

A vicious circle commences; more highways are built for the convenience of the suburbs. These corridors invariably serve as inducements to increase commuting so that the nearby suburbs are overwhelmed by growth and the suburban fringe moves further and further out from the urban center. Traffic congestion increases. The highway planners say more roads are needed. But more roads only increase urban decay and help to erode the city tax base by driving more people out to the suburbs. Meanwhile the traffic jams get worse and worse.

The Chamber of Commerce spokesmen who usually have been stout supporters of highway plans ought to take a long look at what has happened in New York. While the city was building a new skyscraper, the World Trade Center, for use as a corporate office building, corporations were leaving the city for greener places. In the past four years, some two dozen large firms have moved headquarters or major facilities out of New York. These companies include such giants as General Dynamics, American Can, Corn Products Co., Olin Mathieson and Avco. As this book was written, the parade was joined by General Telephone and Electronics Corp., Continental Oil, Shell Oil, Stauffer Chemical and at least a dozen others. The pattern has been repeated throughout the nation, particularly in such cities as Detroit, Chicago and Boston.

The trouble is that when such corporations move out to the suburbs, even more troubles result. Seldom, if ever, are these residential communities properly constructed or planned to accommodate explosive business and industrial growth. Seldom does a labor market for these businesses exist in the suburbs. Moreover, low cost housing for lower-income workers is often an impossibility. The decentralization of urban sprawl by farsighted, carefully planned new communities oriented to business and industry developments is an optimum goal. You would have what Mrs. Rooney was calling for, a community in which people lived and worked. Moreover, efficiencies could be worked out in the production of power and heat as well as in innumerable other ways. But moving out of the city into a community of an already established character is quite another matter. Maybe this community should have broadened its social and economic base long ago, but it is questionable whether moving a business out of the city, *without very thorough planning for innumerable possible side effects,* is going to bring constructive change.

The authors are not trying to create the impression that

transportation problems are the sole reason for the death of cities or for the flight of commercial and industrial interests from the cities. Certainly there are other factors such as the crime rate, inferior educational opportunities and the general breakdown in municipal services. However, a strong case can be made that all these problems originated when cities were turned into service centers for communities that could be reached conveniently by car. Indeed, in 1968 the Koerner Commission found that inadequate and inhuman transportation systems that imprisoned millions of people in ghettoes and destroyed traditional urban character had been a major underlying cause of the wave of riots that beset the nation's large cities in the summer of 1967. Nor do the authors of this book gloat over the move away from cities by corporations: this will only result in merely shifting the basic problem to some other ground. Like Mrs. Rooney, we are calling for a return to the community concept, the great centers where our commercial, intellectual and spiritual lives intermingle. And along with the brave adventures in new town-building presently underway, the place to work this concept out is in the cities.

The Massachusetts Task Force

At the state level, one strong foe of the highway lobby has been Massachusetts' Governor Francis Sargent. Sargent came into office during a storm of major proportions over proposed new interstate segments for Boston, including an inner loop that would have displaced some 1300 houses in relatively poor neighborhoods. Sargent ordered a road-building moratorium while the metropolitan area's transportation needs were studied by a special task force on transportation.

That task force, composed of ten men with extremely wide-ranging experience, was mandated to analyze how present highway plans affected jobs, housing, community life and the environment and how alternative modes of movement had previously been overlooked.

In a preliminary report to the governor, the task force

concluded that 1) public transportation services had suffered drastically on account of the federal government's emphasis on highway construction, 2) that local street traffic and parking problems were never considered by expressway planners, 3) that highway plans were seldom integrated with existing or planned, public transit facilities, 4) that highway plans made no provision to replace demolished housing, 5) that the planners made no provision to replace open space used by their roads, and 6) that there was a "total absence" of studies showing the impact of environmental pollution.

"Understandable as the present situation is," said the task force report, "we can no longer tolerate a decision-making process characterized by fragmented responsibility, agency secrecy, citizen distrust, lack of community participation, inter-agency rivalry, and the exercise of political leadership only in exceptional 'crisis' situation."

Halting Progress in Rapid Transit

Boston is far more fortunate than most other cities. Since 1914 it has had a good rapid transit system operating below and above ground with lines extending out into five outlying metropolitan districts. This existing rapid transit system provides a good base for modern expansion.

New York's Metropolitan Transportation Authority boasts that it too has a "going" system with various plans for the future. The MTA was created in 1968 as a superagency incorporating New York's subway system, city and commuter bus services and the trouble-beset Long Island Railroad. It remains to be seen whether the MTA can match its boasts, but few citizens would place large bets on its success at this time.

For that matter, nationwide, rapid transit has not yet been given a real opportunity. Nor has it been properly conceived in terms of an overall transportation picture. Quite a few cities have rapid transit systems on the boards or in construction. In the San Francisco Bay Area, the billion dollar Bay Area Rapid Transit System (BART) is about to open, ballyhooed as the world's first "fully automated train control system," with some

seventy-five miles of tracks running north, east and south of
Oakland and San Francisco.

However, San Francisco's rapid transit along with many
others being planned is *primarily a service for commuters
living outside the central city. There has yet to be a new transit
system built in the U.S. that has as its prime objective the
improvement of transportation within the city so as to make
the city a more enjoyable as well as an economically and
socially viable place to live and work.* Some, if not most, of the
planned systems bypass poor neighborhoods and black
ghettoes or simply fail to provide stations in these areas. San
Francisco has been beset by the sudden proliferation of new
high-rise office buildings which were predicated heavily on the
ability of BART to make the city far more convenient for
commuters. BART has also triggered a wave of land
speculation. So many new housing projects and commercial
developments have sprung up in its path that it is likely that
BART will begin operation with a need to bolster its services
for the suburbs and the more distant exurbs, rather than do
something for the cities of Oakland and San Francisco.

The 1970 Urban Mass Transportation Assistance Act was
hailed by President Nixon as a measure that would lead to a
"significant breakthrough in mass urban transportation"
during the coming decade. However, the bill committed no
more than $10 billion for new bus and subway systems and for
improvements in existing systems for the cities over the next
twelve years. It would take half of that amount alone to finance
the rapid transit improvements that are needed to smooth out
the kinks in New York's metropolitan transportation system.
In March, 1971, the administration proposed a revenue sharing plan that would ultimately channel $2.56 billion to states
and cities to finance "balanced transportation" systems. In a
message to Congress, the president intoned that "we have
relied too much in our cities on cars and on highways, and we
have given too little attention to other modes of travel."
However, while his proposal included measures that would
encroach on federal highway grants and would put grants for
non-automobile-related transportation systems on par with

road handouts, the president steered clear of the Highway Trust Fund on the weak grounds that the interstate system is seventy-four percent completed. Overlooked was the fact that the most expensive uncompleted segments of the interstate system lie in or around urban areas and that the trust fund will continue to generate five billion or more dollars annually during the next three years.

Congressional proponents of rapid transit and other modern means of transportation had hoped that the administration would want to establish an equivalent to the Highway Trust Fund, a regular Trough as it were, that would provide money on a sustained basis for different modes of transportation. Moreover, the president's proposal was keyed to his other revenue sharing plans which have met with strong opposition in Congress and seem highly unlikely of gaining passage. Consequently, while the highway lobby was sure to bark—as it does whenever its sacred prerogatives are endangered—at this writing it appeared that the administration's proposals would face extremely rough opposition among legislators. Of course, it is questionable whether *any* legislative proposal would succeed if it displeased the highwaymen.

During the past several years, any number of new pathways have been charted in order to relieve the urban transportation impasse and make transportation planning an integral—if not the key—element of all community planning. Had San Francisco's BART, for example, been conceived as a means of directing orderly growth and relationships between the city and the exurbs and not primarily as the dream of transportation engineers and land speculators, its attendant problems might well have been forestalled.

The main obstacle in achieving the ideal results with all these new pathways has been the political unattractiveness of any system which does not enrich or fatten one set of interests at the expense of another. We have noted that a strong rapid transit lobby has failed to materialize to take on the highwaymen. Indeed, one risks overemphasizing the importance of rapid transit. Actually, the ideal urban transportation system would encompass a bewildering variety of vehicles—better buses, subways, fast train links inside the city and to points outside, escalators and elevators to move people within or under building complexes, and mini-electric cars and buses specially designed to fit in or connect with shopping arcades and pedestrian malls. The findings of the Center City Transportation Project, a federally backed study by private consultants and engineers, provided a new vision for urban transportation which incorporated all of these modes of transportation. However, little has been done by the federal government to pursue this vision.

There is also a growing movement to make highway projects include all-encompassing provisions for urban renewal and redevelopment made necessary by the new roadways. Redevelopment grants would likely far eclipse highway handouts. The danger here is that urban highways may be justified as part of citywide urban renewal projects which ultimately displace many people, shatter neighborhood values and lead to total chaos in the urban fabric. The more one looks into the vastly complex business of transportation, especially as it affects the state of urban life, and the more one sees the pervasive influence of the highway lobby, the more humble one becomes about suggesting rosy solutions. Yet the description of the problem has inherent in it some general principles, and some imaginative—and desperate—people have given some insight into how we might keep ourselves moving. Some of these principles and proposals are discussed in the following chapter.

CHAPTER 8

TO KEEP MOVING

The dilemma of transportation is an entirely different kind of problem than the energy crisis. The gravity of the energy problem is well recognized by many citizens but solutions appear at the moment impossible to find. At the very least, we need to know a lot more before we can put down solid guidelines for energy policy in the future. On the other hand, locked into the convenience and private comfort of the automobile, we tend to grasp the problems of transportation only when we are caught up in them, only when we are stuck in traffic or are rushing to make a plane connection. However, in contrast to the energy crisis, the solutions to our transportation problems are, by and large, obtainable at the present state of technical knowledge. Major scientific breakthroughs are not required.

Systems for the Cities

It is in urban centers that transportation problems are most visible and most intractable, and it is here that national transportation priorities must be set and quickly implemented. To say, as we have, that cities are "dying" is convenient shorthand but it is not accurate. Cities are systems, not living organisms, and they do not die as all living organisms must. People who live in cities know that they are systems—systems which often cannot be fought. But a city system, properly functioning, provides the truest forms of freedom and mobility. It is when the system gets out of phase that it becomes tyrannical, and most cities are out of phase.

People who live in cities are also inclined to realize that transportation is a *system*. Most other people do not see it that way: we have gone to great lengths to point out the personal nature of the auto-driving, mobile American's view of getting from one place to another. Until the mobile American recognizes that, in his mobility, he is part of a system, and until national and local policy is based on this widespread recognition, there can be no real improvement. Until transportation policy makers at *all* levels have accepted the fact that transportation is a system and not a competition in which highway contractors and automobile manufacturers battle with other modes of transportation, matters will simply get worse. It is in the cities where the need for systematic transportation facilities are most obvious and, perhaps, best recognized. It is to the cities that our attention must first go.

Planners, right up to the present, have shown little flexibility in their view of urban travel. As was stated in a 1968 study entitled *Tomorrow's Transportation,* directed by Charles M. Haar, then with the Department of Housing and Urban Development, "The common characterization of urban transportation modes as a blunt dichotomy between public rail transit and the private automobile is far too simple. Cities are the most pluralistic places in modern society; their citizens need a wide range of travel service, a mix of transportation services carefully designed to meet their varying travel needs."

Haar's team of transportation/urban analysts found that while automobiles presently were more useful and versatile than mass transit systems, which had not been changed for years to meet modern urban conditions, the car is increasingly becoming more of a menace. Moreover, automobile ownership was minimal among those who were most in need of decent means of transport within the city—people in poor neighborhoods and the black ghetto. The quality of employment, education and a host of other necessities was reduced for these people because of their lack of transportation options. "These are the 'captives,' left to use the transit systems or do without," said the Haar report. "If transit service continues to be reduced, many of these non-drivers will be destined to be isolated more and more in their narrow neighborhood worlds while all around them the advantages of automobile mobility benefit the relatively affluent majority more each year."

The HUD study recommended both short and long range solutions. It also noted that technological innovations must not be overemphasized at the expense of economic changes and improvement in the management and regulatory aspects of transportation that up to now have been significant inhibitors. For example, important improvements might result from raising tolls and parking charges during peak traffic hours or from basing routes, schedules, fares, labor practices and various franchise costs on performance incentives.

What might be done in the short term to improve urban transit? The HUD report recommended improvements under several categories. Dealing with the right of way, it suggested that buses, which now carry seventy percent of all urban transportation passengers, be put in reserved or exclusive lanes, or on separate streets. The report also suggests that buses, in general, be given "priority in the traffic stream," for example, by being allowed to bypass toll booths on bridges and freeways. The study suggested new bus designs, cleaner, quieter standard buses, "dual mode" buses that could be automated on track lines or driven over highways and several kinds of large capacity buses. For the automobile, the HUD report suggested rental systems, featuring cars specially designed for urban trips, to supplement mass transit facilities.

What is needed for the long run? According to the federal study a whole new array of automated control and propulsion systems must be developed. One system, conceived as a solution to peak-hour commuter needs, is called the "Dial-a-

Bus." After a commuter telephones for service, a computer sorts out requests and dispatches buses over a predetermined route as bus capacities are filled. You can call the bus from home or from dial-a-bus station phones. The convenience of such a bus system would undoubtedly give it a good deal of business in the off-peak hours as well, a period during which present transit systems suffer a severe financial drain.

Another proposal was a "Personal Rapid Transit" system whereby passengers would activate small two or four person capsules that would travel over an exclusive automated guideway system—the urban ground equivalent of the ski slope gondola.

Dual mode vehicles and moving belts would round out the transportation network of the cities of the future. From every standpoint, technical to economical, these adaptations and major changes will not come about until the federal government expresses a commitment to finance research and development projects for ground travel of the magnitude devoted to moon and space travel during the past decade.

If and when federal and state transportation programs and their attendant subsidies do indeed provide for "balanced" systems in the cities, a host of needs will have to be considered. 1) Rapid transit subways and trains should not be encouraged to serve mainly suburban communities and areas further out. Rather they should be designed to serve traffic within metropolitan boundaries. Rapid transit links certainly should extend to airports outside the cities before they add to the cities problems by increasing the flow of people inbound from a distant exurb. 2) Clean buses—powered by gas turbines, natural gas, electricity and steam—should be given a place, particularly when rapid transit systems cannot be built on *existing* rights of way. The roads that have already been built in cities should be used mainly by public transportation, i.e. buses and taxicabs. 3) Finally, more city mayors should follow the lead of New York City Mayor John Lindsay who has experimented with schemes to ban cars in busy downtown sections and to promote the use of bicycles.

The ban-the-car-downtown movement has gained increasing

support, even from Fifth Avenue merchants who now realize that shoppers are more inclined to be indulgent when they are not maddened by the frustrations of driving and can walk in a leisurely manner down the middle of the avenue.

The New York City chapters of the New York State Society of Professional Engineers have gone so far as to propose that all private cars, taxis and buses be banned for eleven hours every work day between 34th and 59th Streets, and between Third and Eighth Avenues, with certain exceptions for emergency vehicles and essential suppliers. In a special report, the engineers suggested a system of tandem buses and several other measures to take care of commuter requirements within midtown Manhattan.

Along these lines, there are a few short-term possibilities for U.S. cities. Eventually, they even could be tied in with long term solutions. Where they have the authority, cities should impose a differential toll on motorists so that, for example, a car entering a city with four occupants would pay only 25¢ as opposed to $1.00 for a car carrying just the driver. This would work where city centers are accessible through only a few major arteries and bridges. Sales taxes ought to be extended to parking payments as a means of forcing car commuters to share their ride in a car pool or to use public transportation. Cities and suburbs ought to get together to provide parking terminals close to metropolitan boundaries. From these points, commuters could use different means of transportation, ranging from rapid transit and buses to special mini-cars and bicycles. And, in keeping with the historical tradition of the world's foremost cities, American urban authorities ought to create many more areas within their cities where people can walk unmolested by noisy, dirty driving machines.

Bicycles

What follows is a catalogue of ideas—by no means exhaustive—which may be used as partial solutions to some of the numerous problems of transportation. Bicycles lead our list. We firmly predict that bicycle paths will be increasingly proposed and built in cities and suburbs. For years doctors have recommended bicycle riding as one of the healthiest ways to get around. Bikes are not only wonderful for the respiratory and muscular systems of cyclists, but they are also pollution-free. In more and more situations, bikes are becoming one of the fastest modes of transportation as well.

At the start of National Transportation Week, May 16, 1971, John Volpe, DOT secretary, said that he wanted to establish bicycle lanes along the nation's interstate highways. Volpe was among a crowd of dignitaries and public officials who rode bikes that day along the Potomac River, the very route which Volpe also plans to turn into an interstate highway segment.

It is a happy fact that bicycle sales have risen dramatically during the past decade—from less than four million to over eight million. Interestingly, the percentage of adult bicycle buyers rose from fifteen percent in 1970 to an estimated twenty-five percent in 1971. Throughout the country, bicycle clubs, bicycle trail advocates and the bicycle business in general have all enjoyed a remarkable resurgence. Officials in many cities have cooperated in setting aside bicycle tracks or closing off roads for cyclists.

The bike comeback should be encouraged by positive steps on the part of state, local, and federal government parks and transportation officials. The Oregon legislature, for example, passed in August, 1971, a bill directing that at least one percent of all state highway funds be used to construct bicycle trails and footpaths. The state highway department was not enthusiastic, but the public was and the governor signed the bill: An abandoned railroad right of way was selected for the first bike trail.

As an integral part of the urban park system now being planned for federal surplus properties in the cities, bicycle centers should be built with locker and exercise facilities, steam rooms, weight lifting and muscle toning equipment, etc. A bike shop might also be franchised in each center. Emanating from these centers should be a trail system for bikes. People should be able to go to the bike center just to exercise and commuters should be able to use it as a terminal from which they can cycle to work.

State and town governments should get together and provide similar bike centers as well as encouraging private enterprise to take part. Some commuters have already made arrangements on their own to park their cars on the city outskirts where they keep a bike. In Washington, in 1971, it was estimated that 6,000 people rode bikes part of or all of the way to work.

Off-road Vehicles

Dune-buggies, snow-mobiles, all-terrain vehicles and other such machines do not come directly under the purview of this book since they are not, specifically, involved in transportation, as we have defined it—that is, the purposeful carrying of people or things from one place to another. Except in rare instances, they are merely toys—dangerous, noisy and obtrusive ones at that.

As such they have been appropriately barred from many areas. Suffolk County on Long Island, N.Y., has banned beach vehicles from 10 A.M. to 6 P.M. during the summer. They have been banned entirely from the Cape Hatteras National Seashore. Off-road vehicles are restricted in six national parks in California but not in twelve others. Certainly the National Park Service should eliminate them altogether from these few areas of the nation specifically given over to beauty, nature and peace. State parks should do the same. The authors have absolutely no sympathy whatsoever for these vehicles and, perhaps unpopularly, feel that they should be restricted altogether, like any dangerous weapon or public nuisance, with the exception of those people who can demonstrate a legitimate need for them.

Railroads

It is totally illogical and deplorable that the government subsidizes air and automobile travel by paying for roads and airports while it discourages travel by passenger train. It is true, to be sure, that the railroad giants received an extraordinary windfall in real estate when the federal government gave them rights of way during the nineteenth century. But times have changed. Train travel in Europe is a joy. In the U.S. it more often than not a study in frustration.

The French are about to build an experimental "air cushion" commuter train which runs on what looks like a monorail but is actually a cushion of air. It is expected to operate at up to 120 miles per hour and is relatively noiseless, running on an engine known as a linear-induction motor. Meanwhile in various parts of Europe, a reviving rail system—of the traditional kind—is competing hard and well against airlines for intercity passenger business.

No organization has fought harder to save U.S. railroad travel than the National Association of Railroad Passengers. Anthony Haswell, chairman of the Washington-based, non-profit corporation, observed at a senate hearing in 1969 that "one line of railroad track is capable of carrying as many people in the same time span as ten to twenty lanes of highway." He went on to note that wherever fast and efficient train and mass transit service had been provided in the U.S., notably in recent years, the public had responded enthusiastically. He cited evidence to show that in Philadelphia, Chicago, Cleveland, Detroit and Toronto, modern transit service had been successful beyond all expectations. At the same time, NARP distributed to members of Congress and the public a fifteen-page booklet entitled "Save Rail Passenger Service," containing samples of editorials from newspapers throughout the country that argued in support of rail service.

The response to this and other expressions of the need for a resurgence in rail transportation has been the creation of a federally-backed corporation to restore and manage passenger services between the nation's major cities. Amtrak is the name given to the National Railroad Passenger Corporation. It is a quasi-public operation, backed by government loan guarantees and some direct subsidy money. Since opening day, May 1, 1971, its beginnings have *not* been auspicious. (Within six months of its birth, Amtrak was requesting $170 million more in federal funds to keep operating until July 1, 1973.) Travellers who expected to find a "new look" in the intercity trains taken over by Amtrak were disappointed. The inefficiencies and delays, confusion among train and station employees, scruffiness of train interiors, and shoddy food and beverage service that characterized passenger trains in recent years have not been—and perhaps could not have been—changed overnight by Amtrak. Moreover, Ralph Nader charged that Amtrak had effectively abandoned half the existing intercity trains while serving as a government-sponsored front to shoulder the responsibility for the eventual failure of all railroad service.

Indeed, that charge holds much substance. Amtrak was empowered to run only intercity trains, defined by the Interstate Commerce Commission as those running seventy-five miles or more. Amtrak consolidated only a select number of intercity rail operations and did not touch commuter trains which, by their abysmal service, have done much to fill the cities with automobiles.

One need not second-guess Amtrak or point out the efficiencies and convenience that may eventually derive from this consolidation of lines and eventual elimination of others.

Railroad travel and more efficient use of rail service for freight will continue to suffer in the U.S. until the federal government changes its rules. Through a trust fund similar to the Highway Trust Fund, and/or through other means, the Federal Government must extend loan guarantees as well as grants in order to bring about modern, efficient intercity as well as commuter services. In addition, it makes no sense that while a trucking company cannot own a railroad, the Interstate Commerce Act prevents railroads from diversifying into other modes of transportation. This and other strangling government regulations must be overhauled. Indeed, the prestigious President's Council of Economic Advisers has recommended that the ICC itself be relieved of its regulatory power over surface transportation. In February, 1971, the CEA in its annual report to the president, urged that truck, railroad and barge freight rates be set by open competition.

Airplanes and Airports

This small book is no place to go into the unique complexities, both technical and economic, of the airlines and their related industries. No newspaper reader can be unaware that the entire aerospace industry is apparently in deep trouble. Purely from the standpoint of transportation—specifically the movement of people from one point to another—it may be enough to point out that while the Penn Central Railroad was allowed to lapse into bankruptcy in 1970, Congress passed legislation in 1971 to bail Lockheed out of bankruptcy. It is also instructive that in the battle over the SST, the arguments for it had to do almost entirely with the economic requirements of the industry. No serious argument was advanced in favor of the SST as a particularly valuable asset in the simple matter of transporting people from one place to another. The reason for this is obvious.

It is the usual experience of people flying even short distances—between New York and Washington, for example—to spend more time travelling on the ground, going to and from the airport or waiting there, than is spent in the air. Increasingly larger planes have caused increasingly larger traffic jams and delays at all airports. The SST would have only exacerbated a deteriorating situation.

If air travel is to improve, and if it is to fit into a rational system of domestic transportation, it may well be that airlines will have to learn how to think small.

Large interstate airlines are beginning to worry about small *intrastate* carriers who, not regulated by the federal government, can charge lower rates. A notable example is Pacific Southwest Airlines which dominates intercity flights between San Diego and Los Angeles. At an average of 4.7¢ a mile, a passenger does far better than the 12.7¢ a mile for a flight between New York and Boston, even better than the 6¢ a mile between New York and San Francisco. The smaller, intercity airline may indeed flourish elsewhere in years to come.

In 1971, the Department of Transportation and the National

Space and Aeronautics Administration issued a joint report which suggested that among other air transportation priorities, the industry with federal assistance should look more to tailoring air technology to the problem of short-hauls. The median air trip is 600 miles, the report said, and the need for 500-mile trips and less is growing. Yet, it is precisely this kind of short-haul business that is the biggest financial drain on the airlines. While the call for new technology is appropriate, the call for thinking "small," as is the case with Pacific Southwest Airlines, is equally appropriate.

Technologically, one of the serious problems with short-haul, intercity air travel is that the types of planes envisioned as most efficient for this work—e.g. vertical short take-off airlines (VSTOL)—are also likely to be especially noisy. There seems to be progress in this area: Rolls-Royce, trying to get a new lease on life after its sorry connection with the U.S. aircraft industry, demonstrated a new quiet short-take-off engine at the Paris Air Show in June, 1971. A combination of design factors, including a variable-pitch fan, make for higher propulsive efficiency on take-off, less noise, and greater operating flexibility—all of which are problems that have plagued VSTOL efforts so far.

Yet, until very quiet planes and "small economics" are developed, it seems unlikely that intercity or any other kind of air travel can be significantly improved from the standpoint of the passenger.

In addition, the problems surrounding the location of airports and airline terminals must also be resolved. Rapid transit systems must not only play a key role in reducing urban congestion, they must also serve as links to airports—those presently in existence as well as new ones. New Jersey and New York have already cooperated on the future financing and construction of high-speed transit links to Kennedy International and Newark Airports. In the future, new airports must relate to ground transit systems: there is little sense in building any new Dulles-type airports. It takes about an hour's drive and parking time to reach Dulles Airport from downtown Washington, D.C.

Imaginative design of airport and airport-access systems will permit them to be far less intrusive on people and their environments. In a recent battle between environmentalists and proponents of a jetport that was planned for the Florida Everglades, one such imaginative proposal was created but not aired because the debate had so rapidly become locked in an either/or, yes/no controversy. The environmentalists, led by Friends of the Earth, quite properly won the yes/no battle: the jetport has been stopped and the unique ecological properties of the Everglades National Park have been saved from the noisy, polluting intrusion of jet flights. But was this park really saved? And were any alternatives really considered?

In the midst of the battle, Stewart Udall's Overview Group was asked to examine alternative schemes for the jetport. They determined from various ecological and other studies that the real danger posed to the Everglades National Park by a jetport placed to the north of its boundaries came from the kinds of developments that inexorably go along with airports and their access roads. At the same time, another danger to the fragile ecology of the park rests in the fact that lands to the north, where the flow of water through the park originates, are not under the control of the park. In other words, the way to permanently assure the health of the Everglades is to enlarge it. That takes a great deal of money, which is not likely to be forthcoming from Congress in the near or distant future.

The Overview Group, which included the imaginative Gerald Snyder, now financial officer for New York's Urban Development Corporation, proposed an entirely different kind of airport which, they believed, would solve *both* problems of the Everglades. All the terminal facilities such as ticketing, baggage, etc., would be located, conveniently, in the city of Miami. Only the airstrip and hangars would be out in the saw grass. The strip and the terminal facilities would be linked by a uni-purpose rapid transit train which would virtually dump passengers onto their planes. For three dollars, a passenger would be whisked from the Miami terminal along an access route that could never be developed into anything else, to an airstrip that similarly could support no further development, such as motels or even restaurants. Of the three dollars, half would go to a fund for the purchase of additional land for the park. Snyder's cost projections showed that such a scheme would be profitable.

As it developed, the Overview scheme was never truly proposed and, therefore, never fully studied by either economists or ecologists. Yet, in the authors' opinion, it demonstrates the kind of imagination that could well solve some of the problems of locating airports. Indeed, in this way and in others, properly located airports—both commercial and private—can also serve as a means for the preservation of open space not otherwise included in parks or public easements. Clearly, it is desirable to minimize an airport's environmental impact by restricting adjacent development.

Port Authorities should be empowered to take over undeveloped open space in wide areas around airport sites. If the land so condemned was desirable for public recreation, not only would the public receive a new benefit from airport planning but the indiscriminate development that invariably springs up all around airports would also be prevented. Naturally, a recreation facility under or near the glide paths of jets landing and taking off would have its drawbacks, but it would be a lot better than the present arrangement of airports in the midst of residential areas.

Transportation Trusts

It makes no sense to require the governor of a state to spend money received from the federal government out of the Highway Trust Fund solely on more interstate highways, if road systems are no longer the best means of transportation, and if other transportation modes are far more critically needed. Nor should the mayors of major urban centers be subject to the pressures of state governors who use urban interstate construction money as an excuse to continue the flow of federal highway dollars into the state coffers. Superficially, it may seem sensible that highway-related taxes be appropriated for highway-related expenditures. The trouble is that there is no comparable tax method to benefit on a suitable scale the alternative modes of travel and shipping that certainly are of increasing necessary in the U.S.

All transportation tax monies—gas taxes, airline fees, various excise taxes, etc.—ought to go into a single federal transportation trust fund. Grants would be made from this fund only when states presented transportation master plans showing how roads, airports, rapid transit systems and railways would fit overall needs, how much each system was estimated to cost, and what the priorities were in giving attention to different modes of transportation. Federal grants would have to be spent in accordance with a master plan schedule approved by the federal Department of Transportation.

Route Selection

At present, all transportation planners pay far too little attention to the selection of routes that will comply with environmental criteria. As previously noted in this book, all too often highways split neighborhoods, run through parks and become noisy, intrusive corridors creating health dangers and invading the privacy which we all need a certain amount of.

State highway departments and the federal Department of Transportation should have to comply with comprehensive criteria, before highway grants are awarded. Simple, cost-benefit analysis, based mainly on engineering considerations best-suited to rural road systems, must be dropped in favor of analysis based on social factors, regional and area-wide planning goals and natural resource and environmental protection. In other words, a highway should not destroy or degrade settled neighborhoods or historic buildings and places. A highway should be part and parcel of master plans for a region's growth and land use. A highway should not directly result in pollution nor should it encourage land use and growth patterns that threaten land, water, air and other natural resources. As expressed most effectively by regional planner Ian McHarg and his associates in a proposal for an interstate road segment between the Delaware and Raritan Rivers in New Jersey, "The highway is thus considered as a major public investment which will transform land uses and values and which will affect the economy, the way of life, health and visual experience of the entire population within its sphere of influence."

A Citizen Lobby

A recent novel, *Cedarhurst Alley,* told the story of a man who bought a house on Long Island and somehow realized only afterwards that he was on a major flight path to nearby Kennedy International Airport. After all forms of relief from the noise failed, rather than sell out, the hero bought a World War II dirigible and arranged to fly it on Labor Day weekend at the end of a 1500-foot cable over what he claimed was his air space. To be fair to the airlines, he warned them of his plan on the Friday morning of the holiday weekend by running a full-page advertisement in the *New York Times.* As an afterthought, he put a coupon in the ad soliciting names in support of his lone battle. In this comic—and compelling—story, the balloon went up, the planes stopped, the national guard was called up, the balloon was shot down by a fighter plane, and by Monday the hero had lost. But on Tuesday he found that thousands of similarly afflicted individuals had sympathized with his ad and had sent him money—enough to start a real lobby. There is, the novel hypothesized, a huge constituency of anti-airport-noise people to be mobilized.

The number of people who are afflicted by the slow-down in mobile America and by the increasing hassles brought on by a transportation system gone awry is *truly* enormous. It includes even those who, like most of the poor, have no transportation at all to speak of. The question is, of course, how does one mobilize this huge constituency?

Certainly it takes more than an ad in the newspaper, though that fictional account is an obvious echo of the very real and very effective newspaper ads of the Sierra Club in the 1960s against the Grand Canyon dams. Perhaps a citizen lobby for transportation awaits a singular individual like David Brower of the Sierra Club. Brower is undoubtedly one of the men who moved the conservation movement out of the realm of "kooky" birdwatchers and dull photographs of contour plowing in fifth grade textbooks. He gave the movement great appeal and shoved it into the modern world of concern for the environment. The time was ripe then for a Brower, and he was not alone. The time may be ripe now for a similarly energetic national movement which would take transportation out of the realm of sheer self-interest and dreary statistics.

Meanwhile, the most effective citizen action has been and will continue to be at the local level. Coalitions of citizens from greatly different backgrounds and interests, neighborhood groups, towns, county-wide organizations—all have played key roles in forcing officials to think again about a planned highway or a new airport. These efforts have served mostly as delaying tactics, just as was the case with early conservation actions. Yet when citizens dig in their heels, they *can* force public officials to listen to rational alternatives. And it can happen more quickly than one would imagine.

The success of a group in the Boston area called the Greater Boston Committee on the Transportation Crisis is a cheerful case in point. Over a period of ten years, academicians, suburbanites, black ghetto dwellers, housewives, professionals and conservationists all have joined together and developed the expertise and clout to stop an inner-city loop, the expansion of Logan airport, and other highway plans. More important, they have forced politicians and bureaucrats to look at rational alternatives for building a transportation system in the Boston area. While Boston has always been different from the rest of the country, these efforts are reproducible.

Some Basic Desire Lines

As in all such matters, the goals of a transportation system are a question of priorities. To the authors, it does not seem that making it easier for larger numbers of affluent easterners to fly directly to Hawaii for a three-week vacation should take precedence over the needs of a ghetto-dweller to cross a city to his place of work in less than two hours.

Mobility, Washington's Angela Rooney has said, is a right. It is, furthermore, a necessity. It can also be a pleasure. If priorities are set in such a way that the urgent necessities are dealt with, it may be that the pleasures which the mobile American has always sought in motion itself can be restored as well. It is such a pleasure to take the train in many parts of Europe that it seems fairly possible that a reviving rail system may replace much intercity air travel on the continent. Some San Francisco commuters are enjoying themselves on a new ferry—not only "getting there" but smugly watching the traffic jams develop on the bridge overhead. Other San Franciscans still enjoy the particular cameraderie of riding the famous old trolleys—and they are "getting there" too.

As things are presently, *some* mobile Americans can go nearly anywhere. For most of these people, getting there is a nightmare, but escaping may seem worth the bad trip. Among the results is that what once was the frontier has become a recreational colony. Natural resources—from fuel to wilderness areas—are disappearing down the mobile American's gaping gas tank and many of the last redoubts of natural beauty have been invaded and nearly destroyed. Meanwhile, in the cities, getting to work or going someplace for pleasure is becoming more difficult and less efficient than at the turn of the century.

If humane transportation systems were to grow, taking root first in our car-choked cities, we believe it would be a significant step in making American communities so much more attractive as places to live and work in. We believe that as a result a great number of the mobile American's trips would become unnecessary. And then Americans—any American—would be truly mobile and, to that extent, free.

APPENDIX

APPENDIX A

Consolidated Edison Company of New York, Inc.
4 Irving Place, New York, NY 10003
Telephone (212) 460-2003

July 22, 1969

The Honourable John V. Lindsay
Mayor of the City of New York
City Hall
New York, N.Y. 10007

Dear Mayor Lindsay

In recent weeks representatives of our Company have discussed publicly the urgent need to construct 1200-1600 MW of new fossil-fired electric generating capacity to meet New York City's power needs in the years 1974 and beyond. They have discussed, also, the possibility that this new generating capacity be provided by enlarging an existing generating station in New York City.

Our conclusion, after examining the alternatives, is that we can best provide this essential new supply of energy for New York City by enlarging our existing plant at Astoria. We are convinced we can plan this enlargement to protect the environment of our City. The key to reconciling the construction of new generating capacity in the City with environmental goals lies in the recent development of a new grade of fuel oil which is almost free from sulphur.

As fuel for the new generating capacity, we propose to use very low sulphur fuer oil (0.37%); and the boilers will be designed so that they can also burn natural gas as fuel when it is available. We are prepared to seek Federal Power Commission approval for the use of natural gas when and if it becomes available. At the present time natural gas is not available in the required volumes.

We further propose, if assured supplies of very low sulphur fuel oil can be obtained at prices fair to our customers, to convert the existing generating units at Astoria from low sulphur coal and fuel oil (1% sulphur) to very low sulphur oil (0.37% sulphur). This conversion, if we are able to make it (and we are optimistic that we can), would reduce the air pollution from the enlarged Astoria Plant to a point substantially below that caused by the existing plant. Specifically, if we can obtain 0.37% oil for all the Astoria units, the enlarged plant, including 1200-1600 MW of new capacity, would emit approximately 60% less sulphur dioxide and 55% less fly ash than are released by the existing plant. The use of this very low sulphur oil for the entire plant would go beyond existing legal requirements which permit the burning of fuel oil containing almost three times as much sulphur (1%) in existing equipment. We propose, however, to retain the present coal-firing equipment at Astoria as a precaution against an interruption in the supply of very low sulphur oil, all of which probably would come from foreign sources.

The proposed construction of additional electric generating capacity at Astoria is consistent with the Memorandum of Understanding entered into between the Company and the City in 1966. At that time, Con Edison pledged to the City of New York to make every effort to meet certain clean air goals by the year 1976. In brief, these goals were to reduce the particulate matter emitted from our plants by 64%, and to reduce emissions of sulphur dioxide by 71%. New fossil-fired units built within the City were not excluded but the Memorandum did state, in part, that "Consolidated Edison accepts the principle that, to the fullest possible extent, power from coal or oil fired plants should be generated outside the City limits and brought into New York by transmission lines." At the time the Memorandum was entered into, the sulphur content of the oil burned in New York City generating plants was well over 2%, and the sulphur content of coal was about 1.4%. We believe we have complied fully with the Memorandum of Understanding, and, in many respects we have done more to reduce air pollution than required by law.

To place in proper perspective our plan to enlarge the Astoria plant, I think it proper to review the current status of our overall plans for (a) supplying the increases of 350 MW of electric power required each year by New York City and Westchester County, and (b) retiring our oldest and least efficient generating units now operating within the City.

To supply the additional power required by our customers each year, and concurrently to reach the clean air goals for 1976, Con Edison for several years has been engaged in a program of building nuclear and hydro-electric generating stations outside New York City. In good faith, and at great cost, the Company has attempted to carry out this program. Since 1963 we have attempted, and we are still attempting, to obtain a license to build the 2,000 MW Cornwall pumped-storage hydro-electric project. In 1965 the Company contracted with the Westinghouse Corporation to build a 1,000 MW nuclear unit at Indian Point on the Hudson River. In 1967 it contracted with the Westinghouse Corporation to build another 1,000 MW nuclear unit at Indian Point. In 1968, the Company purchased from General Electric and Associated Electric Industries the principle components for a fourth nuclear unit to be constructed near Indian Point. This imaginative and costly program—if completed on schedule—would have met the load growth of New York City and Westchester (and- enable us to meet our clean air goal for 1976. By substituting more efficient generating capacity for many of our old generating units, it also would have reduced our average cost of generating electricity.

For reasons beyond the control of Con Edison, this program has encountered serious delays. The 2,000 MW Cornwall hydro-electric project, originally scheduled for completion in 1967, is still before the Federal Power Commission because of persistent opposition from the Scenic Hudson Preservation Conference and associated groups. When I joined Con Edison in August 1967, Cornwall was scheduled to go on the line in 1972. This schedule has now been delayed until about 1977.

For different reasons, the two 1,000 MW nuclear units which Westinghouse is building for us at Indian Point, called Indian

Point No. 2 and No. 3, have fallen behind schedules. When I joined Con Edison, the scheduled completion dates in the Westinghouse contracts for Indian Point No. 2 were June 1969 and for Indian Point No. 3, June 1971. We are now advised that No. 2 probably will not be on the line until after the summer of 1970, and that No. 3 probably will not be finished until the Spring of 1973. Based in part upon this experience, we doubt that we can complete Nuclear No. 4 before 1976.

Obviously these delays and uncertainties have left large gaps in our power planning. We have moved as fast as we can to fill them. At a cost of about $80 million, we are installing an additional 750 MW of gas and light oil-fired turbines at our Astoria and Gowanus Stations. These machines are designed primarily for peaking power, their fuel (light oil) is expensive, and they are not as reliable as hydro-electric units. But they have the virtue that they can be built quickly—in about 2 years compared to 4-5 years for a conventional fossil-fired plant and 6-7 years for a nuclear plant. With the recent slippages in the construction schedules of Nuclear 3 and 4, we have had to move quickly.

Twelve months ago we began active negotiations with Central Hudson Gas & Electric and Niagara Mohawk Power Corporation to build an oil-fired plant called Roseton on the Hudson River near Newburgh, New York. The cost to Con Edison will be approximately $70,000,000 plus the cost of transmission. From this we expect to receive 480 MW by the Summer of 1973. We also agreed with New York State Electric & Gas to purchase 600 MW from its Bell nuclear station on Lake Cayuga in 1973, 1974 and 1975. But on April 11, 1969, New York State Electric & Gas announced the indefinite postponement of this plant because of unresolved environmental problems.

On May 19, 1969, we entered into an understanding with Orange & Rockland Utilities, Inc. to acquire 400 MW of a 600 MW plant which it proposes to build near Haverstraw on the Hudson River. The cost to Con Edison will be approximately $60 million, plus the cost of transmission. The estimated completion date is late 1972 to early 1973. Our further efforts to develop a source of power supply outside the New York City metropolitan air shed, with suitable transmission arrangements, and reasonable assurance of availability in 1974, have not been successful.

To fill the remaining gaps caused by unavoidable delays in our program, we must construct new oil and gas-fired generating capacity of about 1,200-1,600 MW for completion in 1974 at the latest. We should not, and cannot, continue to rely indefinitely on 40-year-old generators to meet a substantial part of New York's power supply.

I had hoped that the next time we proposed a new generating unit in the City it would be nuclear, without a smokestack. But our first duty to New York City is to provide it with sufficient energy to maintain the economy of the City and Westchester County, and the delays we are encountering with our Hudson River pumped storage and nuclear plants are beyond our power to prevent. In fairness, too, there are important counterbalance considerations which favor a proposal to enlarge Astoria. Three years ago, Con Edison could obtain only fuel oil with a sulphur content of well over 2% and it was not even certain that fuel oil with as little as 1% sulphur could be obtained. Today we are confident that we can obtain enough 0.37% sulphur fuel oil for the new capacity, and probably for the entire Astoria Plant, and we have already obtained 1% sulphur oil and coal for our existing units.

It is also important to note that, even with the addition of new oil- or gas-fired capacity at Astoria, Con Edison will attain the goal set in cooperation with the City in 1966 of reducing the particulate matter (fly ash) emitted by our plants by 64%, and reducing emissions of sulphur dioxide by 71%, by 1976. I am enclosing a revised "Ten Year Program to Meet Growing Energy Needs and Reduce Air Pollution, 1969-1979". It spells out the details of how we now intend to reach this goal. Also, it schedules for retirement all the electric generating units at Hell Gate, Kent Avenue and Sherman Creek as well as certain units at East River, Hudson Avenue, Waterside, 59th Street and 74th Street.

I do not wish to conclude this letter without reaffirming our faith in nuclear energy as the energy of the future. We have one nuclear generating station in operation, and two more under construction at Indian Point on the Hudson River. Last month we applied to the U.S. Atomic Energy Commission for construction permits to build two nuclear stations at Verplanck on the Hudson River. For future construction of nuclear stations, we have required David's Island in Long Island Sound.

We firmly believe that nuclear energy, in combination with pumped storage, holds the greatest promise of enabling Con Edison to supply the immense new quantities of electric energy required by New York City and Westchester County with the least impact on the quality of the environment.

We hope and trust that those individuals and groups who are concerned about protecting the quality of our environment will lend active support to the nuclear energy program. We particularly appreciate the support you have given this program. To the extent that the nuclear program lags, the growth in energy requirements must be met by the construction of more fossil-fired generating plants.

Sincerely

Charles F. Luce

P.S. Subsequent to preparation of this letter, we have received additional indication that planned future purchases may not be available on dates previously expected, specifically short-term purchases of up to 310 MW for delivery beginning in the summer of 1970. We have therefore decided to advance the completion date of 300 MW of previously planned additional gas turbine capacity from 1971 to 1970; and to purchase another 150 MW of gas turbine capacity for completion by 1970. This will increase the gas turbine peaking capacity on order from 750 MW to 900 MW. The attached revision of our ten year program reflects this change in plans for new gas turbine capacity.

APPENDIX B

(This section is a detailed amplification of points made throughout the section on energy; it is reproduced from *Electric Power and the Environment* and serves as an excellent manual in itself for utility planners and those concerned about, or affected by, power plant proposals.)

Environmental Protection Checklist and Guidelines for Site Selection

All steam-electric plants as well as other installations using fossil or nuclear fuels will have some adverse impact upon the environment. However, with proper studies and appropriate design, much can be done to reduce such impacts. The purpose of this chapter is to set forth a general guide of the factors that should be considered and the pre-construction and post-construction studies that should be undertaken to assure that plant sites are selected and planned so as to minimize the adverse effects upon the environment. It should be recognized, of course, that each site is unique and that the general guides must be adjusted to meet the requirements of the particular site.

These guides, presented as environmental protection checklist together with an indication of minimum standards for site selection, cover the following areas of concern: (1) land use planning and appearance of facilities, (2) water quality protection, (3) air quality protection, (4) control of radioactive wastes, and (5) noise control.

Land Use Planning and Appearance of Facilities

Steam-electric plants should be located as near as possible to load centers and adjacent to adequate cooling water supplies.

Fossil-fueled plants should also have access to adequate fuel supplies. A first requirement in preparing a land use plan for a proposed plant site is the availability of sufficient land area.

Guidelines

Common to all plants is the requirement of adequate land area for the plant, switchyard, cooling facilities where necessary, and for plant expansion where planned. Coal fired plants require large acreages for fuel storage, ash disposal, and air quality control equipment. A fossil-fueled plant with 3,000 megawatts capacity may require in the range of 1,200 to 1,600 acres if coal fired, 200 to 400 acres if oil fired, and 150 to 300 acres if gas fired. A cooling pond would require an additional 1 to 2 acres per megawatt of capacity.

Siting criteria for nuclear-fueled power plants have been developed by the Atomic Energy Commission on the basis of public safety. Part 100 of Title 10, Code of Federal Regulations, provides criteria for determining an exclusion area surrounding a proposed plant, a low population zone immediately surrounding the exclusion area, and a population center distance representing the distance from the plant to the nearest boundary of a densely populated area containing more than about 25,000 residents. The plant owner must have authority to determine all activities within the exclusion area, including exclusion or removal of personnel and property from the area. A 3,000-megawatt nuclear plant would require a site ranging from 300 to 500 acres in area. For light-water plants a cooling pond would need to be about 50 percent larger than that for a fossil-fueled plant of equal size.

The physical characteristic that must be considered in locating a power plant include the geology, seismology, hydrology, and meteorology of the proposed site. These are factors that are evaluated by the AEC before it approves a proposed nuclear plant site. However, the flexibility of siting may be increased by providing engineering safety features in the plant design to compensate for the natural characteristics of the site. The relationship of the plant site to historical, archeological, and cultural sites must also be considered.

In developing a land use plan for a proposed site, careful consideration should be given to existing developments in the area and to existing zoning regulations. The location and design of facilities should be such as to minimize the impact on the natural environment. Esthetic treatment can be enhanced by the establishment of buffer zones around the plant. These zones can be used to screen the plant facilities by means of trees, vegetation, and other landscaping.

The esthetics of a power plant can be improved by good architectural design and landscaping treatment. Strategic profiling and positioning of buildings and structures, use of appropriate materials and colors, and use of screening and blending of landscaping are among the techniques available to moderate visual impact. It is important also that proper consideration be given to the visual effect of transmission lines extending from the plant.

Where practicable, the construction of a thermal power plant should provide beneficial additions to the recreation facilities of the area. In some cases, heated cooling water can be diverted to swimming lagoons or pools. In some areas, sport fishing may be enhanced by the discharge of warm water into a water body. Cooling ponds may provide opportunities for public boating, picnicking, and camping. The exclusion area of nuclear plants may provide camping areas for scouts and similar groups.

Nuclear plants in general can be more attractive than fossil-fueled plants. To take full advantage of their inherently better esthetic qualities, nuclear plants should include imaginative architectural landscaping and suitable recreational facilities other compatible land uses. In some cases, information centers established at or near plant sites may be desirable. Animated displays and exhibits on atomic energy with emphasis on safety may be featured.

Environmental Protection Checklist

Consistent with the guidelines discussed above, there follows a listing of factors to be considered in site selection relative to land use planning and esthetics of facilities.

1. *Land Area and Population—*

(a) Area—Sufficient acreage should be provided for planned facilities, including future expansions. For nuclear plants, the area under control must meet AEC regulations in 10 CFR 100.

(b) Population—The relationship of nuclear plants to population centers must be in accord with AEC regulations in 10 CFR 100.

2. *Physical Characteristics of Site.*—The suitability of the site should be determined by the following types of studies:

(a) Hydrologic—To determine ground water gradients and chemical characteristics, interchange between surface and ground water, and soil permeability as a basis of plant design; to determine incidence of inundation of site by floods, tsunamis, or hurricane-driven tides.

(b) Geologic—To determine the underlying soil and/or rock to establish foundation criteria.

(c) Seismologic—To analyze the site seismology characteristics to establish seismic design criteria.

(d) Meteorologic—To determine the susceptibility of a site to winds of hurricane or tornado force and the local diffusion climatological patterns for use in plant design.

3. *Relation to Historical, Archeological, or Cultural Areas.*—Consideration should be given to the proximity and effects on these areas, which are listed in the National Register of districts, sites, structures and objects significant in American history, architecture, archeology, and culture.

4. *Land Use Plans—*

(a) Consistency with State and Regional Land Use Plans—The plant site should conform with adopted state and regional land use plans. To the extent possible, utilities should participate in future land use planning.

(b) Consistency with Area Land Use—Site use plans should conform generally with adjacent land uses, now or planned, and with zoning regulations in the area.

(c) Other Uses of Site—Full consideration should be given to recreational and other compatible uses of the plant site. Also, consideration should be given to the need for visitor centers and other facilities to accommodate the visiting public.

5. *Esthetics.*—Architectural Treatment—The architectural design should recognize the engineering requirements so that the plant exterior can reflect the functions of the facility and at the same time convey a pleasing and uncluttered appearance that blends with the surrounding area.

The appearance of the installation can be improved by the provision of a buffer zone around the plant, the judicious positioning of buildings on the site, and the use of screening and blending landscaping.

Water Quality Protection

Guidelines

An important factor in selecting and planning the use of a thermal power plant site is the type of cooling water system to be used. Where adequate water supplies are available, and such use does not degrade the quality of the water below approved water temperature standards, once-through systems are used. Sources of water for such systems include rivers, lakes, reservoirs, estuaries, and the ocean. Where adequate water quantities or flows are not available for once-through use without violating approved water temperature standards, cooling ponds or cooling towers must be provided. In such systems, which may be used for complete cooling, partial cooling, or to supplement once-through systems during certain periods, the water is recirculated and only sufficient makeup water is needed to replace losses by evaporation and blowdown. All cooling water systems should be designed to avoid or minimize adverse heat effects on the receiving body of water.

Under provisions of the Water Quality Act of 1965, the states are charged with establishing water quality standards, including temperature criteria, for interstate and coastal waters, subject to approval by the Secretary of the Interior. Administration of this program is by Interior's Federal Water Pollution Control Administration. The standards are established on the basis of proposed uses of the water. The thermal criteria generally consist of maximum permissible temperatures and maximum permissible changes in temperature, normally to apply outside of an allowable mixing zone. Enforcement of approved standards is the responsibility initially of the states with back-up authority in the federal government. In addition to criteria for interstate and coastal waters, many states have established standards for intrastate waters.

In order to minimize the impact of cooling water use on water bodies and assure compliance with approved water quality standards, a number of pre-construction and post-construction studies are needed. These studies should begin at least two years before plant construction is scheduled in order to properly design the cooling water system and predict the impacts of cooling water use on environmental and biological conditions of the water body. Comparable monitoring studies should continue for at least two years after plant startup in order to verify the effects of plant operation on the water body. Control techniques should be established for operation in accordance with design criteria, and appropriate monitoring should continue during the operation of the plant.

Studies of a water body proposed as a source of cooling water supplies may include measurement of wind direction and velocity, measurement of current patterns in water bodies, measurement of temperatures and other physical and chemical properties of the water, algal studies, macroinvertebrate studies, and fish studies. The biological studies, which should be carried out under the direction of aquatic biologists, should take proper account of seasonal factors and should identify unique or significant forms.

The flow and current patterns in a water body are important in determining the dispersion of the heat load and extent of the mixing zone. Streamflows of many streams are measured by the U.S. Geological Survey. Measurements at additional sites may be made by using the USGS gaging techniques. Currents in water bodies may be measured by current meters. Such current surveys may be particularly important when waste heat is to be discharged into an estuary. Flow patterns in estuaries and other water bodies may also be determined by using dyes or isotope tracers. Post-operational aerial surveys of heat discharges to water bodies using infrared techniques may be useful in predicting the heat dispersion patterns of proposed plants.

Measurements of the properties of the water should follow standard procedures such as those in Standard Methods for the Examination of Water and Wastewater, 12th Edition, American Public Health Association, and might include determination of: temperature, turbidity, biochemical oxygen demand, hydrogen ion concentration, and the content of coliform bacteria, dissolved oxygen, nitrogen, and phosphorus.

Algal studies should determine the population of both free floating (phytoplankton) and attached (periphyton) species. Samples collected with a net equipped with a metering device (such as a Clark-Bumpus net) or a metered pump, should be taken at the bottom, mid-depth, and surface levels near the proposed points of water intake and discharge to determine the quantities present. A midsummer and midwinter 24-hour sampling program should disclose any diurnal vertical migration and the effect of thermal stratification on vertical movement of these organisms.

Macroinvertebrate surveys using Peterson or Ponar dredges should be made to determine the type and numbers of species. The presence of large numbers of such organisms, representing the middle group in the aquatic community, indicates that they have available microscopic organisms for food and, in turn, can provide food for fish. Samples should be collected from selected stations for each type of bottom material found within or immediately adjacent to the expected area of artificial temperature change. Collection of samples from these stations should be made four times per year, preferably coinciding with the midpoint of the seasons. Radioactivity analyses should be made of captured animals as well as of bottom deposits.

Studies to determine fish populations and seasonal variations in population can be made by the use of gill nets, trap nets, trawls, shoreline seines, and sonar methods. Properly selected sampling stations should be established for such surveys. Use may also be made of a sampling type quantitive creel census carried out on a periodic basis. The fish studies should include a survey of spawning areas.

The prediction of temperature changes in the receiving waters is complicated by many factors affecting heat transfer to the environment. Mathematical models are being developed to predict the dissipation of heat to the atmosphere and the dispersion of heat in a water body after receiving the cooling water discharges. The availability of digital computers facilitates the consideration of the many factors and changing conditions involved.

Hydraulic models are useful in determining the likely mixing and recirculation of plant effluents. Temperature measurements may be made on the models and, after comparison with prototype observations, they may be used to appraise temperature changes in the environment, particularly in the mixing zone. Hydraulic model studies can assist in the assessment of likely water movement, stratification, and mixing processes. Such studies are also useful in designing the cooling water systems, including the planning of intake structures, canals, outlet structures, and dispersion facilities.

Environmental Protection Checklist

Following is a checklist of site selection factors relating to the protection of water quality.

1. Selection of Cooling Water System—

(a) Once-Through Systems—Used where sufficient cooling water is available to keep within approved temperature criteria and avoid any significant adverse effects on the receiving water body.

(b) Cooling Towers—Used to meet water quality standards where water supplies are limited, for complete cooling, partial cooling, or to supplement once-through cooling during certain periods.

(c) Cooling Ponds—Used where needed to meet temperature limits of receiving waters and sufficient land area is available at relatively low cost and makeup water supplies can be provided.

(d) Reuse of Water—Increased reuse of water can be anticipated, including use of sewage and industrial treatment effluents.

2. *Hydrologic Studies*—

(a) Streamflow—To determine available average and firm flows in streams to be used to supply cooling water.

(b) Current Patterns—To determine dispersion characteristics, particularly for estuarine areas.

3. *Physical and Chemical Properties of Water.*—Using standard techniques, measurements should be made of the following items as appropriate:

(a) Suspended Solids

(b) Dissolved Solids

(c) Alkalinites

(d) Turbidity

(e) Total Coliform Bacteria

(f) Fecal Coliform Bacteria

(g) Dissolved Oxygen

(h) Biochemical Oxygen Demand

(i) Hydrogen Ion Concentration

(j) Conductivity

(k) Chlorides

(l) Organic Nitrogen

(m) Ammonia Nitrogen

(n) Nitrite Nitrogen

(o) Nitrate Nitrogen

(p) Total Phosphorus

(q) Soluble Phosphorus

(r) Temperature

4. *Ecological Studies.*—Such should be made before and after plant startup to determine their seasonal variations and the effects of plant operation.

(a) Algal Studies—To determine species and quantities present at proposed points of intake and discharge of cooling water supplies.

(b) Macroinvertebrate Studies—To determine type and numbers of species present.

(c) Fish Population Studies—To determine species and numbers present and those being caught.

(d) Unique Systems—Identify any unique or significant ecosystems.

5. *Temperature Prediction Studies.*—These studies are necessary to demonstrate ability of cooling water systems to meet water temperature criteria.

(a) Mathematical Models—These studies take into account site conditions, proposed plant operating factors, and known physical relationships to predict the changes in temperature and dispersion of waste heat in receiving bodies of water. Digital computers are usually employed in such studies.

(b) Thermal Hydraulic Models—These studies are useful in determining the likely mixing and recirculation of plant effluents.

6. *Design Studies.*—These design studies of cooling water systems make use of data collected at the site and may utilize both mathematical and hydraulic models.

Air Quality Protection

Air quality protection requires consideration of present and potential air environmental conditions and how these would be affected by planned operation of generating plants. Thus, serious consideration must be given to the air pollution potential in selecting the sites for fossil-fueled steam-electric plants. Such plants contribute substantial portions of certain contaminants found in the atmosphere, such as sulfur oxides, nitrogen oxides, and particulate matter. The availability of desirable fuels, such as natural gas and low-sulfur coal for utility use is limited. Supplies of low-sulfur residual fuel oil are increasing on world markets, but they fall short of the potential demand and their use is limited largely to plants where supplies can be delivered by water transport. Despite the research under way and the apparent initial success of a limited number of processes in prototype installations of removing sulfur oxides from stack gases of coal burning plants, large-scale operation has yet to be demonstrated. Thus, no large-scale process for such purpose is readily available to utilities.

The Air Quality Act of 1967 provided an intergovernmental program for the prevention and control of air pollution on a regional basis. To put this program into operation, the Departmen of Health, Education and Welfare is required to designate air quality control regions and issue air quality criteria and reports on control techniques. State governments are then expected to establish ambient air quality standards for the air quality control regions and to adopt plans for implementation of the standards. The ambient air quality standards and implementation plans must be submitted to HEW for review and approval. If the states fail to act or their proposed air quality standards are considered inadequate, HEW may establish appropriate standards. Enforcement of the approved standards is primarily the responsibility of the states with some backup authority in HEW. Administration of this program is by HEW's National Air Pollution Control Administration.

Guidelines

The air pollution potential of a particular site depends upon a number of factors, including the characteristics of the fuel, the emission control measures incorporated in the plant design, the stack height, the exit velocity of the flue gases, the topography of the site, and the meteorological conditions in the area. The air quality control standards in effect may influence the choice of plant locations.

Factors related to air quality requiring appraisal in site selection include population distribution, expected growth pattern, existing or expected local industrial pollution sources, terrain over the area of stack gas dispersion, and land-use patterns such as for agriculture, forestry, or recreational purposes. With the present level of technology, a mine-mouth plant in remote, undeveloped, flat terrain might be desirable. However, adoption of national ambient or emission standards would reduce the advantage of such sites.

Meteorology is important to the design of air quality control systems of a plant. Meteorological measurements should include the prevailing wind directions and velocities, ambient temperature ranges, precipitation values, and factors related to temperature inversions.

Studies of a proposed plant site should include an air monitoring program which would begin at least two years prior to plant construction and continue after the plant is in operation. Each air monitoring station should include such instruments as an aerovane wind direction and velocity recorder, recording thermometer, Davis sulfur dioxide analyzer, Gelman particulate sampler, dust fall jar and lead oxide candle, and provision for measuring the coefficient of haze.

Data collected from air sampling stations at operating plants, including meteorological data, can be used to verify the mathematical models used during plant design to predict air quality at specified locations. Also, measurements of the amounts of fuel burned per unit of time, combined with measurements of the carbon dioxide content and temperature of stack gases, give an indication of combustion efficiency.

Determination of expected ground level concentrations at various distances from the plant site with varying stack heights is most important in evaluating air quality effects from potential power plants. By dispersing and diluting stack gases before they reach ground level, tall stacks can play an important but incomplete role in air pollution control. Using appropriate formulas and coefficients, such as those from the American Society of Mechanical Engineers' guide for tall stacks, it is possible to estimate the maximum ground level sulfur dioxide concentration which may be expected from a plant where sulfur dioxide emission and stack height are defined. In designing stacks for a particular site, however, use may be made of wind tunnel studies considering the topography of the site and expected meteorological conditions.

Environmental Protection Checklist

The following checklist includes site selection factors relating to air quality protection.

1. *Area Population and Industry—*

(a) Population—Determine present population distribution and expected growth patterns.

(b) Industry—Determine existing and expected industries in the area and likely emissions to the air.

2. *Site Conditions—*

(a) Topography—Consider factors of topography affecting dispersion of air emissions.

(b) Meteorology—Make measurements of prevailing wind directions and velocities, ambient temperature ranges, precipitation values, and factors related to temperature inversions.

(c) Air Monitoring—Provide for air monitoring before startup and after plant operation, measuring wind direction and velocity, temperature, sulfur dioxide content, nitrogen oxide content, particulate content, dust fall, and haze.

3. *Air Quality Criteria—*

(a) Standards—Design and operate facilities to meet applicable air quality emission standards for the plant.

(b) Monitoring—Provide monitoring methods adequate to determine how plant operating emissions conform to any applicable ambient air quality standards.

4. *Design Factors—*

(a) Stacks—Design the stacks to provide optimum dispersion of stack gases consistent with Federal Aviation Administration regulations concerning stack heights in the area.

(b) Particulate Control—Install facilities necessary to provide optimum control of particulate emissions.

(c) SOx and NOx Control—Consider expected composition of any fossil fuel planned for use (coal, oil, or gas). Depending upon the included sulfur content, consider best available technology for possible removal of sulfur exceeding proper tolerance level. Pending availability of commercial processes for plant site removal of sulfur, consider use of low sulfur fuel and provision for future plant modification to remove sulfur from normal fuels. Nitrogen oxide control depends on further development of usable processes and equipment.

Control of Radioactive Wastes

For the light-water reactors which are expected to be used predominantly for nuclear power plants for the next 10 to 20 years, neither the reprocessing of fuel nor the disposal of radioactive wastes is conducted at the plant site. However, small controlled quantities of radioactive wastes are released to the atmosphere and the adjacent waterway.

Guidelines

In the operation of a nuclear reactor, radioactive wastes are accumulated as solids, liquids, or gases. Solid wastes are placed in shielded containers and shipped to disposal centers. Liquid wastes are kept in holdup tanks to permit decay of their radioactivity to a lower level and treated by ion exchange and evaporation equipment, but some small amounts of radioactivity are released in the liquid effluent. Gaseous wastes are filtered and kept in holdup tanks to permit decay of their radioactivity to lower levels, after which they are released to the atmosphere in controlled quantities that can be accurately measured. Thus, some radioactivity is released in liquid or gaseous form to the plant site environment.

The Atomic Energy Commission requires, as part of applications for construction and operating permits, detailed analysis of all safety problems and plant design and operating techniques to cope with them. The AEC regulations establish strict limits on the release of radioactive wastes. These regulations are set forth in Part 20 of title 10, Code of Federal Regulations. Normally, waste disposal is not an important factor in site selection if the reactor facilities can meet the requirements of these regulations. It could be of importance, however, if large installations are planned for locations on the same waterway or in the same airshed.

In order to assure compliance with regulations governing release of radioactive materials and to guard against radiation hazards, a program of radiological monitoring must be established. The levels of background radiation in the environment should be established by measurements taken over a period of at least two years prior to plant operation. These measurements must be used in determining the allowable limits of regulated releases of radioactive wastes. Monitoring of radiological effects on the environment should continue during plant operation to control radioactive waste discharge and to check on the effectiveness of in-plant measurement of releases.

In order to measure possible plant effects, two types of sampling stations should be established. One type, as indicator stations, would be placed where maximum radiation attributable to the plant would be expected. The other type, to measure background radiation, would be placed where radioactive levels of less than one percent of levels at indicator stations would be expected when the plant is releasing a significant fraction of allowable releases. Sufficient samples should be collected and analyzed to assure that significant pathways of radioactive materials to man are evaluated. The samples taken should include air particulates, precipitation, external radiation, milk, and well water; also water, sediments, fish, and benthos from the receiving water body.

Environmental Protection Checklist

Following are site selection considerations relating to control of nuclear wastes.

1. *Allowable Waste Releases*—

(a) AEC Regulations—Criteria for determining allowable radioactive waste releases are set forth by 10 CFR 20.

(b) Determination of Proposed Releases—Based on AEC regulations and site conditions, including background radiation, meteorological characteristics, and related factors.

2. *Measurements for Design.*—Through analysis of safety questions and the related engineered safeguards and operating procedures, methods for protection of the environment must be built into the plant. Such analyses and designs will require measurements and studies necessary to predict the effects of project construction and operation on the environment. Such studies may require the use of digital computers.

3. *Monitoring Programs.*—These must be developed to guard against hazards to the environment and to assure

compliance with applicable regulations. Stations should be selected to measure radiation where maximum effects of the plant operation are expected and also where background radiation can be determined. Measurements should be made on the following materials sampled in the region of the site to determine the level of radioactivity.

(a) Airborne Dust
(b) Precipitation
(c) External Radiation
(d) Milk
(e) Receiving Waters and Sediments
(f) Receiving Water Benthos
(g) Receiving Water Fish
(h) Estuary Oysters
(i) Well Water

Noise Control

Control of noise from fossil-fueled generating stations has become increasingly important with the use of larger units.

Guidelines

Sound control measures appropriate for the nature of the surroundings should be taken. Plant noise can be disturbing at substantial distances from its source, and the effect of sound levels upon the entire surrounding neighborhood must be considered. Ambient noise levels should be measured as part of the site selection process and used to establish criteria for noise attenuation in the design of the plant. Future development of adjacent properties must be anticipated in order to incorporate proper isolation during the initial design phases. Analysis should be made of the sound generating potential of plant equipment.

Environmental Protection Checklist

The following site selection factors relate to problems of noise control.

1. *Site Studies*—
(a) Ambient Levels—Measurements should be made of

existing ambient noise levels to establish a baseline to determine the contribution of the proposed plant to noise levels.

(b) Projected Area Development—Consideration should be given to expected future developments in the area that would contribute to noise levels.

2. *Monitoring Studies.*—Ambient noise levels should be measured after plant startup to determine the plant's contribution to noise levels and to test the effectiveness of attenuation designs.

BIBLIOGRAPHY

In addition to the books, articles, and reports cited below, the authors have gathered information, opinions, and ideas from numerous interviews and conversations with individuals cited in the text and some who are not. A considerable amount of information has been and continues to be found in the pages of newspapers, notably the *New York Times,* the *Washington Post,* and the *Wall Street Journal.* The weekly magazine, *Science,* published by the American Association for the Advancement of Science, reports regularly on these and other environmental matters with special skill and authority. A source of semi-technical but extremely well-written information on these matters—with a useful trans-Atlantic perspective—is the weekly British magazine, *The New Scientist.*

ENERGY

Abrahamson, Dean E., *Environmental Cost of Electric Power.* New York: Scientists' Institute for Public Information, 1970.

Baldwin, Malcolm F., "Public Policy on Oil—An Ecological Perspective." *Ecology Law Quarterly,* Summer, 1971.

Clark, Wilson, "How to Harness Sunpower and Avoid Pollution." *Smithsonian* Magazine, November, 1971.

Commoner, Barry; Corr, Michael and Stamler, Paul J., "The Cause of Pollution," *Environment,* April, 1971.

Conservation Foundation. *Your Right to Clean Air.* 1970.

Consolidated Edison Company. *Annual Report.* 1970.

Council on Environmental Quality. *Annual Report.* 1971.

Federal Power Commission. *Testimony before U.S. Senate Commerce Subcommittee on Energy, Natural Resources and the Environment.* January 30, 1970.

――――――――――――. *Opinion No. 584.* Granting Consolidated Edison a license to build pumped-storage unit at Cornwall, New York.

――――――――――――. "A Review of Consolidated Edison Company," *Power Supply Problems and Ten-Year Expansion Plans.* 1969.

Federal Water Pollution Control Administration, Pacific Northwest Laboratory. *Industrial Waste Guide on Thermal Pollution.* 1968.

Jones, William K. *Second Interim Report on Load Shedding Procedures of Electric Corporations in Times of Emergency: Consolidated Edison.* Report of New York State Public Service Commission, May 24, 1971.

Landsberg, H. and Schurr, S. *Energy in the United States: Source Uses and Policy Issues.* Resources for the Future, 1968.

Legislative Reference Service, Library of Congress, Environmental Policy Division. *Economy, Energy and the Environment.* Joint Atomic Energy Committee, September, 1970.

Lodge, George C., "Top Priority: Renovating Our Ideology." *Harvard Business Review.* September-October, 1970.

National Academy of Sciences, Committee on Resources and Man. *Resources and Man.* San Francisco: W.H. Freeman & Co., 1969.

Office of Science and Technology. *Considerations Affecting Steam Power Plant Selection.* December, 1968.

――――――――――――. *Electric Power and the Environment.* August, 1970.

Stein, Jane. "A Hot Debate Generated by Hot Water." *Smithsonian Magazine.* June, 1971.

Study of Critical Environmental Problems. *Man's Impact on the Global Environment,* Cambridge: Massachusetts Institute of Technology Press, 1970.

U.S. Senate Commerce Subcommittee on Energy, Natural Resources and the Environment. *Environmental Effects of Energy Generation on Lake Michigan.* March 30, 1970.

U.S. Senate Committee on Interior and Insular Affairs. Research Material and Hearings concerned with *A National Fuels and Energy Policy Study,* 1971.

U.S. Congress, Joint Committee on Atomic Energy. *Environmental Effects of Producing Electric Power.* Several volumes of transcriptions. 1969.

Working Committee on Utilities, *Report to the President's Council on Recreation and Natural Beauty,* 1968.

Zeldin, Marvin, "Audubon Black Paper #1, Oil Pollution." *Audubon Magazine.* May, 1971.

TRANSPORTATION

Baldwin, Malcolm F. *The Off-Road Vehicle and Environmental Quality.* The Conservation Foundation, 1970.

Boorstin, Daniel J. *The Americans: The National Experience.* New York: Random House, 1967.

Burby, John. *The Great American Motion Sickness.* Boston: Little, Brown & Company, 1971.

Carnegie-Mellon University. *Advanced Urban Transportation Systems.* Proceedings of Conference held May 25-27, 1970.

Conservation Foundation. "What Is the Role of the Highway in Society and the Environment?" *C-F Newsletter.* June, 1970.

Creighton, Roger G. *Urban Transportation Planning*. University of Illinois Press, 1970.

Department of Health, Education and Welfare. *RID Plan for Unconventional Low Pollution Vehicles*. 1969.

Department of Housing and Urban Development. *Tomorrow's Transportation: New Systems for the Urban Future*. 1968.

Department of Transportation. *The Freeway in the City*. 1968.

Environmental Protection Agency. *Auto Pollution Emissions Regulations*. June 30, 1971.

Halprin, Lawrence. *Freeways*. New York: Reinhold, 1966.

Hapgood, David. "The Highwaymen," *Washington Monthly*. 1969.

Heywood, John B. "How Clean a Car?" *MIT Technology Review*. June, 1971.

Kelley, Ben. *The Pavers and the Paved*. Donald W. Brown, 1971.

Kneeland, Douglas E. "From Tin Can on Wheels to the 'Mobile Home.' " *The New York Times Sunday Magazine*. May 9, 1971.

Leavitt, Helen. *Superhighway-Superhoax*. Ballantine, 1970.

Lupo, Alan, Frank Collord and Edmund P. Fowler. *The Politics of Transportation in Boston and the U.S. City*. Boston: Little, Brown and Company, 1971.

Macinko, John. "The Tailpipe Problem." *Environment*. June, 1970.

Rae, John B. *The Road and the Car in American Life*. Massachusetts Institute of Technology, 1971.

Robinson, John. *Highways and Our Environment*. McGraw-Hill, 1971.

Roberts, Paul O., Jr. and Donald N. Dewus. *Economic Analy-*

sis for Transport Choice. A Charles River Associates study. Heath Lexington, 1971.

Stone, Tabor R. *Beyond the Auto.* Prentice-Hall, 1971.

Task Force on Transportation, *Report to Massachusetts Governor Francis Sargent.* January, 1970.

U.S. Senate Commerce Committee Staff. *The Search for a Low-Emissions Vehicle.* 1969.